WHO OR WHAT WERE THEY?

Alan Godfrey

West Yorkshire Police Constable (retired)

Who Or What Were They?

ISBN 978-1-78808-159-7

DEDICATION

I dedicate this book to my wife, Kathryn, who has been my best friend for over 25 years. Without her support and encouragement across those years I could never have written these words. She has been a rock.

ACKNOWLEDGMENTS

In memory of my late friend and colleague police constable Malcolm Agley. A true and loyal support through the darkest days by my side. I was proud to know him. Rest in peace my old buddy.

I also wish to thank my grandson *Jack Cougill,*12, for his spectacular artwork on the cover. It captures the spirit of what happened long ago.

And *Jenny Randles* for helping me to put this book together. I wrote the words but not necessarily in the right order and she even translated a few of them into English, whilst sharing many of her case investigations from around these parts.

My gratitude goes to *Bob Coates* for bravely coming forward to describe his own account confirming things that happened to us both on that strange night.

Finally, thanks for *Harry Harris* and *Mike Sacks.* Had they not interviewed me all those years ago then nobody would have been any the wiser regarding my encounter.

CONTENTS

INTRODUCTION

Climbing up the slippery railway sleepers holding back a mountain of loose coal, I reached the top and peered over the rim.

What I saw next would haunt me for the rest of my life.

I was no more than inches away from the face and staring into the open eyes of an obviously dead body.

Of course, I had seen bodies before during my service in the police but this one was inexplicably terrifying.

In fact it sent a shiver down my spine.

Those eyes staring up at me seemed to draw me in, as though they were trying to tell me something. And in those moments I thought about the last sight that this poor man must have witnessed.

Why did that image produce such a chill inside? This was a question that would long stay with me.

Little did I know then how those few moments would change my life and eventually embroil me within one of the biggest cover ups by the British authorities about which the file to this day remains 'Classified'.

It was a cover up that would also end my career in the police. Indeed, my story would reach its climax where it had begun ten years earlier - at the police headquarters in Wakefield, West Yorkshire, England.

Stepping outside on that final day as an officer into bright sunshine the heavy door swung shut behind me with a thud. I took a deep breath and must admit that a tear probably appeared on my eyes as I walked across the car park towards my car.

'*This is it*', I thought with a sigh of regret.

It felt strange not being a policeman anymore. I had been one for so long and loved the job. Indeed it had become such a big part of my life.

So how on Earth was I going to cope?

I then had three children to support, a mortgage that needed paying and all the other things that life throws at you. All of these thoughts raced through my head in those frightening moments as I stood on the edge.

For a while I just sat in the car thinking of my predicament and watching other officers milling back and forth as the police headquarters went about its important daily business.

But not for me – not after this day - I had just had my final interview with the DCC (Deputy Chief Constable), who had thanked me for my service and the contributions that I had made to the valley community where I long patrolled.

He also reminded me of the two commendations' that I had received during my career. The deputy chief further remarked that the conduct assessment imprinted onto my file would rate me as having been '*exemplary*'. A slight smile tinged with pride briefly appeared on my lips at his awareness of such recognition.

Then the DCC spoke words that were so unexpected they left me stunned.

He said them quietly but with evident exasperation:

"Alan - Why could they not let sleeping dogs lie?"

What did my commanding officer mean by such an odd question?

And *who* - or *what* - were '*they*'?

Thirty five years have passed since that day of my departure and the search for answers has continued unabated despite many roadblocks placed in my way.

I have pursued this quest whilst inspired by my good friend and colleague PC Malcolm Agley - who sadly passed away just prior to this book being completed.

Malcolm's long held desire was to discover what happened, and to find out why those events took the nasty course that they did. This book would never have been written without him and I dedicate it to his memory because of his loyalty, support and friendship throughout those traumatic times.

Finally I am able to put into print what really occurred all those years ago and let you try to decide what it means for yourself.

First, though, we must return to the very beginning and start a journey which has many twists and turns, some of them down blind alleys and others along paths that might lead to enlightenment.

There will undoubtedly be parts in my account that you will find hard to believe or possibly even unable to comprehend.

I know this because I have been there before you and felt all of those frustrating emotions.

But remember that the story you are about to read shares one thing with a phrase that I would often affirm when acting as a servant of the law.

This book may seem quite extraordinary, even out of this world – but I can promise you this. What I am about to tell you - like when I swore evidence in court. :-

Is the truth, the whole truth and nothing but the truth.

CHAPTER ONE

It seemed like a good idea at the time

Todmorden is a bit of a mouthful, so most of us locals call it 'Tod'. But don't let that make you think this is some backwater town because that is far from the truth.

It nestles amidst three Pennine valleys on the old Lancashire / Yorkshire border which runs right through the middle of the town hall and Centre Vale cricket ground with its adjoining park.

This sometimes confuses outsiders (especially southerners) given the historic links with both counties. Indeed the postcode is OL, from Oldham, Lancashire, but for administrative purposes Tod is very firmly inside West Yorkshire.

This was once a thriving cotton mill centre aided by flowing streams that cross the Calder Valley which can also bring flooding to occasionally plague the town.

However, Todmorden is famous for some interesting things - not least the fact that two Nobel Prize winners were born, raised and educated here.

Sir John Cockcroft was awarded the prize in 1951 for Physics, for being one of men to first artificially split the atom aiding development of nuclear power. His safety features on the Windscale reactor has saved lives.

Then in 1973 the second local Nobel winner was Sir Geoffrey Wilkinson in recognition for his work on the chemistry of complex compounds, which today help in the fight to create successful cancer drugs.

Remarkably, both of these men were taught by the same science teacher at Todmorden Grammar School.

The town can also boast two famous cricketers who were born here and later starred for England. They were Derek Shackleton and Peter Lever, both fast bowlers who, having started in the Lancashire league early in their careers, then played county cricket for Hampshire and Lancashire respectively.

But Todmorden lad Neil Cowie probably reached the highest achievement in sport, playing Rugby League with the all-conquering Wigan side in the 80's and 90's before winning the world cup for England and numerous other medals along the way.

Rock stars also figure in Todmorden's hall of fame. One local being John Helliwell - a member of one of the biggest groups on the planet - 'Supertramp' - with massive hits around the world including 'Breakfast in

America'. And another was the late Keith Emerson, founder member of Glam-rock group 'The Nice' before moving on to form the great 'Emerson, Lake and Palmer' in the eighties and nineties.

Tod even had one of the most famous big band leaders as its son - Geoff Love - who was never off our screens in the eighties and was a recipient of that famous 'Red Book' on television's 'This is your Life'.

Another Todmordian was best-selling author William 'Billy' Holt who wrote scores of books including '*I haven't unpacked*' and '*Wizard of Wirlaw*'. He travelled the world on his famous white horse 'Trigger' and was a regular on TV.

The town itself has been the 'star' in two police based TV series made by the BBC. The popular 1980s serial *Juliet Bravo* was set and filmed in the hills around here. More recently the award winning and hard hitting *Happy Valley* has been based in the Calder Valley with locations at both Todmorden and the moors thereabouts hosting scenes from this much lauded drama.

It was to this colourful town that my parents moved our family from Oldham in the 1950's crossing the Lancashire border to set up home in the first of two 'Fish and Chip' shops that they owned.

One was in Halifax Road which had belonged to my father's uncle and then some years later we moved into Brook Street Fisheries, from where older locals might still remember my parents.

I was six years old when we made the short 15 mile journey and yet to my young class mates at Roomfield

Infants and Junior school I still spoke with a funny, almost foreign, accent!

One particular word that the Todmorden school kids would make fun of me about was *bus* - which if you come from Lancashire is pronounced with a Z, not an S, sound – making it like *buzz* instead of *buss.* But there were lots of other little things that caught their attention and soon got noticed by the headmistress Mrs Rogan – such as the fact that my elder brother Colin and I wore clogs with iron soles and we could make sparks with them just by scraping on the floor.

This party trick did not go down too well with the school head but the kids loved it and they came out with a right Yorkshire phrase that I still use today:- '*Slur thee clog'* meaning 'Slow down' or 'take it easy'.

One day I can remember Mrs Rogan sending for my mother after she had witnessed a fight between me and another lad. I had got hold of him around the back of the neck and by then was kicking him repeatedly on his shin bone, making him cry in pain. All because he had called me '*specky four eyes'*, thanks to the awful NHS clinic glasses that I wore. They made me resemble that nerd-like 'Milky bar kid' from the famous TV ads.

I explained that it served him right for giving such cheek! However, it allowed Mrs Rogan to tell my mother to have the iron soles removed from the offending footwear and replaced with rubber ones. Mum duly obliged, but it was never the same in the schoolyard after that - though possibly a bit safer for my mates.

Having finished my school days at Scatcliffe Secondary Modern in 1962, without gaining any qualifications, I started out on my journey of life as an adult becoming an apprentice Butcher at Dewhurst's located on Halifax Road. These premises are now occupied by James Stansfield & Sons and are the only butchers shop left in town not at the indoor market.

However, when I first started work here there were more than ten of them in Tod centre alone, plus more in that market. Like in so many small towns the big supermarkets have had a devastating effect on family stores, indeed on all the little corner shops that were dotted around most streets.

Just travelling up Halifax Road from the bridge at Key Syke Lane I can think of fifteen shops that are no longer used for any business today. Few now remember 'Duckworths' and also the Co-op at the end of Richmond Street. Todmorden having been one of the earliest adopters of the co-operative movement in the 19th century after it famously was set up to bring cheaper food to the impoverished working classes in nearby Rochdale.

Yes the town has certainly changed - for the worse in my opinion - with its life and soul drained away and much character lost because so called 'forward looking' people in decades past were determined to have their say on how it should evolve.

In my view they all failed miserably and are still doing so to this day! Many towns across Britain would have given their right arm to have the wonderful assets that we had with a towering stone viaduct crossing above it and the canal running right through its midst.

Those with true foresight would probably have built a large marina so that all the canal boats could tie-up and their occupants enjoy a day of sightseeing around the town. It could have had shops, bars and café's situated around it, bringing a 'holiday resort' atmosphere and much needed revenue.

What did our 'masters' decide to do instead? They built an overly large medical centre on the site most ripe for development, when they could have located that building more usefully on the old doctor's site, just across from the main bus station. Placed here it would have been ideal for the more infirm patients to have easy access and freed up the canal side for something imaginative.

Still, despite these disappointments, this is the town that I came to call my home and where my dramatic story was about to unfold.

After I qualified as a butcher I had left 'Dewhurst's' and started to drift from job to job and, indeed, even left the town for a while in 1968 to be with my parents who by then had moved to live on the Isle of Wight.

It was on that island off the south coast that I first entered the world of crime and punishment when I joined the Prison Service. Soon after I was transferred to London and the tough Wandsworth jail and my first child – a baby daughter - was born in the capital before we decided to move back home to Todmorden in 1972.

I left the prison service when I relocated north and now worked for Yorkshire Metro for a couple of years before moving on to Alan Cooper's cabinet making business. And this was where I was first approached by the force about signing up with the Police.

"Have you given any more thought about joining, Alan ?"

This question was posed by Guesty, a young police constable who I had known since he arrived in Todmorden from Doncaster a few years earlier.

We were in the tap room of the old Weavers Arms on Blind Lane playing cards. In those days it was mainly a man's pub. It had a stone floor with an open fire grate which in winter roared and crackled so much that you could have roasted potatoes on it. The wooden tables were long, the tops of which were scrubbed daily. I remember many a happy hour spent in there playing cards, mainly Don and Crib, but with the occasional game of dominoes.

In those long gone days I used to love listening to the old guys that went in the Arms and delighted in hearing the tales that they would tell. These stories were fascinating and sometimes really funny. I can still think back now and see old Sid sat there – a real character and a half.

Sid was an outdoor worker with a windswept ruddy face and cracks deeply etched into his skin by the Yorkshire 'breeze'. He smoked like a trooper and swore as prolifically as any navvy – and could have had an argument in an empty room and still managed to lose.

His sparring partner during most of these disagreements was Tommy, a bespectacled gent, who like Sid loved to get involved in any topic flying around the tap room . He was one of those that had 'been there, done it, and got the T shirt.' Though in reality these two were really good friends who usually ended up agreeing with one another. Oh boy, did we chuckle with them about that.

I was a bit reluctant to give Guesty an honest answer to his important question about my joining the force – as – yes - I had given it lots of thought. But I was also quite worried that my younger more wayward days would prove to be a problem .

As a teen I had been a bit of a tearaway around Tod that saw me get into many a scrape with the local constabulary and I feared that could prove a bit of a problem if I attempted to sign up as one of them.

These incidents were nothing serious and mainly just involved the odd scrap with rival gangs from other towns. But I was convinced that these youthful escapades would go against me, so I did not see the point in pursing such ambitions.

Despite these concerns, Guesty was very encouraging and in the end I asked him to bring the forms to our house and we would see where that led.

I lived on Adelaide Street at the time, a typical terrace of stone built, two-up two-down properties with a large attic room. It came with the then obligatory out door loo and stone flagged back yard. We had moved there from Crescent Street, our first house bought for just £400 after returning to Todmorden from London.

Given how as a Prison Officer I had served at a notoriously hard jail you might think that this in of itself would be such good training that it would all but provide straight passage into the police.

You would be wrong. The prison service then was very different from the police. The penal authorities did not seem too bothered about whether or not you had any close shaves with the law when young as long as you did not have a criminal record – and I did not. In fact the rougher and tougher you had once been in many ways the better suited you were to work in a prison.

Things have changed enormously since the 1970s – as these days you seem to need a university degree in some obscure subject and they might even prefer you to know how to hug a tree rather than look after yourself. But back then the prison service was looking for men that the convicts could understand and relate to. And – yes – they were *convicts* , not inmates like the politically correct brigade would call them today.

To work in a jail they wanted people that spoke the same language as the cons and could handle themselves in any tough situation that might arise. A prison officer was a person who was feared, not so much in a physical sense, more in the power that he held over those under his charge. His word was final and you never argued with it. Prisons were run with an iron fist without any of the modern day hand wringing nonsense.

Con's were only allowed a bible and three library books in their cells - no television, no radio and certainly no phones. They were even forbidden any form of time piece or watch. What they were permitted to do instead was to write three letters a week. They also had to dress the same - grey with blue striped shirts - and their hair must maintain a regulation crew cut.

Surprisingly, given what you might think with such a strict regime, very few assaults on staff occurred back then, unlike in today's 'correctional facilities'.

Guesty arrived later that evening at our house alongside a police sergeant. After helping me to fill in the forms to apply to join the force and generally discussing the job of a police officer if I was selected, they went away and I did not hear anything for a very long time. In fact it was such a protracted silence that I had forgotten all about it by the time that I did.

I was still working at the furniture manufactures as a mature apprentice cabinet maker and had been there now for about two years. I enjoyed the job and the lads in the shop were great. We all used to have a good laugh. In fact at one stage I became the shop steward for the department negotiating bonuses and getting the right piece rates for the items that we were manufacturing.

Then – one day – I arrived home from work and out of the blue found a letter from the recruitment department of the West Yorkshire Metropolitan Police addressed to me.

I did not immediately open this official looking post as I was still unsure what my reaction would be to whatever it had to say.

A part of me wanted to be a policeman, but the other half was less certain. Yet I also did not want to be disappointed if I had been turned down. So it was all a strange cocktail of emotions fermenting in my head - and I just left the letter sitting there for ages.

Having eaten my tea, which had not gone down very well, due to the fact my stomach was turning over with these various possibilities, I decided I would go and have a bath first, as I always tended to do after my evening meal.

I took the letter upstairs with me and started to run the bath. As the water noisily poured behind me I sat on the edge and stared at the letter, trying to see if I could read what was inside the envelope.

This was daft really, but I bet many of you have done the same with an important letter that could change the course of your life.

So this response from the force remained unopened right until the following morning, teasing me and worrying at me – until finally I just thought, what the hell, you need to know what it says - and so I finally opened it.

On my way to work I had a huge smile on my face after reading the contents. I could not tell anybody yet – though - because it merely asked for me to attend at Wakefield Police Headquarters at a given time and date.

At the HQ I would then have to sit an exam, have a medical and face an interview - so it was a step forward but nothing more than that as yet.

So why did I have such a smile on my face? Simple really, I was laughing at myself for being a daft sod and not opening the letter. I kept that smile all day.

I did wonder what my work mates thought of all this secrecy as the next few months seemed to drag by. Days felt like weeks as I waited for the appointment in Wakefield which seemed to be an eternity away.

Then finally that big day arrived. I parked my car in the very same car park that I would sit in a decade later after my life had collapsed around me – but this first time I was feeling very different emotions to those to come later.

Right then I was nervous and unsure whether to continue my quest to join the police because what was about to happen could change everything and I was quite happy in the job that I was doing.

But I had a word with myself and realized that there was nothing to lose by giving it a try. So I took a deep breath and in I went through the heavy oak doors that smelled of polish and gave the whole place a feeling of grandeur – especially with the thick and extremely large doormats that lay atop the tiled floor.

My feet made an echoing sound as I walked along the corridors - still wearing that wry smile etched upon my face. I remember thinking *– by 'eck - you could not sneak in here unnoticed!*

There were about twenty of us sat in a rather large room all politely positioned in front of little desks in small rows slightly apart from each other. It really was like being back at school. We completed all the written exams: - maths, English and spelling included, and ended with one exam that I really enjoyed - an observation test.

This final examination involved looking at various figures and detecting the odd one out or concluding which shape would come next in a sequence. All these challenges were done against a scary ticking clock. It was like Countdown on steroids.

After a small break for tea and biscuits, the number of applicants had been significantly reduced by this stage of the recruitment process to under half those who had first sat down .

Then we survivors were sent for our medical and again the number was reduced until there were only about five of us left for the final part of the selection procedure - an interview with the panel.

I only discovered that I had passed this last stage when, after the interview, I was told to go for a uniform fitting and then given my collar number PC 3961.

After that I was desperate to get home and tell everybody that I was going to be a policeman!

Very soon I was on my way to Bishopgarth police training centre in Wakefield for the week long induction course. I was taking my first steps to becoming a fully qualified copper. Here they pushed your fitness with lots of physical training and marching. We had a drill sergeant who loved to scream in your face and call you all the names under the Sun. He could be very intimidating and if he spotted a weakness would exploit it, picking on you to break your spirit.

Some of the females on the course found his methods too severe and complained, but thankfully the 'pc' brigade amongst the 1970s trainee PCs was not up and running at the time! This was all about honing your strength and ensuring that you had the character to endure.

Our sergeant was a large man and you would not want to get on the wrong side of him, Of course this was all an act. If you could not hack this kind of pressure at the training stage, then let's face it, you would never be any good as a police officer once out in the real world!

I was one of the lucky ones, because I had been through all this before in prison officers training school, so I knew what to expect as did the ex-military personnel who were with me on the course. For all of us 'old hands' this bravado was familiar territory.

There was one incident that I still laugh about today. I had twisted my ankle during a rigorous physical training exercise and it was strapped in bandages. As a result I could not wear my police issue boots. Every morning we had to parade in front of the drill sergeant who inspected our uniform looking for any blemish. In particular these boots had to be polished like glass.

God help you if you failed that inspection, you could find yourself sweeping the parade square or doing twenty laps round it in full dress uniform.

Well that day I turned up for parade already sporting that full dress attire but wearing one highly polished boot and one slipper. At first the drill sergeant did not notice my fashion *faux pas* – but - to my horror – that very day he was accompanied by the school commandant, a chief superintendent.

As they walked the line, closely inspecting every officer, dread came over my face as the sergeant approached me and then stared with horror into my eyes:

"*What the fuck are you doing on my parade square*" he bellowed.

He loomed over me so close that I felt the spit from his mouth entering my eyes.

" *Get off, you moron!*" he screamed.

There was a deathly silence as I tried to hobble off as quickly as I could.

Looking back from the comfort of years I can laugh now, but back then it was an experience that I could have rather done without.

At the end of that week, we were marched through the streets of Wakefield to the local magistrates court were we took the Queen's Oath and found ourselves sworn in by the chairman of the bench ready to serve the realm. We sighed with relief as we had officially made it this far.

Now all we had to do was receive our warrant cards and prepare for thirteen weeks at Dishforth - the police training centre in the wilds of the north Yorkshire moors.

It was part of a then operational RAF camp which included an active runway. Indeed this base still flies Lynx helicopters as part of the Army Air Corps. At Dishforth we would undergo the most intense physical and mental training you could imagine.

The next thirteen weeks would really sort the weak from the strong. But I had no idea when arriving that two decades before my sojourn that this location had hosted strange events that were going to intersect with my own destiny in a most unlikely manner.

On the morning of 19 September 1952 during a 12 day Cold War NATO exercise known as Operation Mainbrace a bizarre incident took place over the field – according to the story that is told in files compiled by the Ministry of Defence and released many years later.

At 10.53 on that bright clear morning several officers and men at nearby RAF Topcliffe observed a Meteor jet landing at Dishforth whilst it was being pursued by an unidentified object. This UFO was bright, silvery and top shaped and was seen to swing in the sky like a pendulum before starting to rotate.

Fortunately we have more than just the Air Ministry file on this event released in 1983. We have the testimony of one of the key men charged with investigating the matter at the time.

He was the private secretary to Air Chief Marshall, Sir Ray Cochrane – then deputy head of the Air Force. His secretary was a civil servant - Ralph Noyes - who a decade later would be promoted to run the division at the MoD tasked with investigating all UFO sightings.

By the time he retired Noyes had become convinced that UFOs were real and befriended investigator Jenny Randles, who, as we will see later in this book, became closely involved in my story around the same time that she first met the now elderly Noyes.

The former MoD man helped Jenny persuade senior politicians to make enquiries for her about major cases and assisted research in other ways. He also revealed the background to those events at Dishforth.

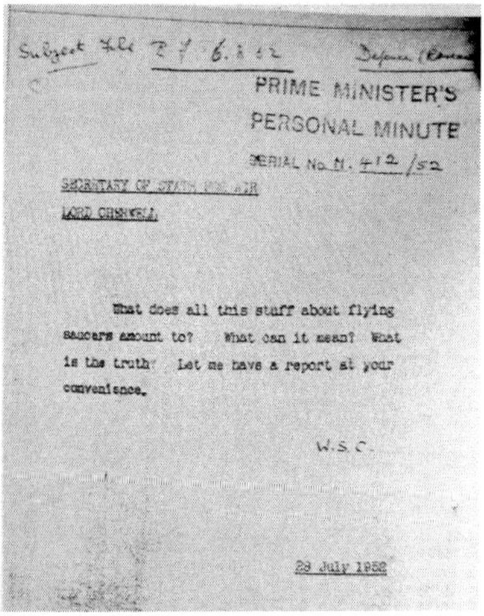

PRIME MINISTER'S
PERSONAL MINUTE
SERIAL No. M. 412/52

SECRETARY OF STATE FOR AIR
LORD CHERWELL

What does all this stuff about flying saucers amount to? What can it mean? What is the truth? Let me have a report at your convenience.

W.S.C.

28 July 1952

His boss, Cochrane, was in 1952 briefing the Air Minister on behalf of Winston Churchill, then serving his last term as prime minister. Reports of UFOs were appearing in the press daily that Summer and after seeking advice from the US Pentagon Cochrane reported that there was nothing to worry about although nobody there seemed to have a clue what UFOs were.

Winston Spencer Churchill penned the above memo to them sent via his air minister Lord Cherwell. He was clearly seeking better answers. Using his initials – WSC – the prime minister asks for an explanation as to what '*all this stuff about flying saucers*' means. He required a detailed report to come back to him from Cherwell.

Just before Churchill had sent that memo Washington DC was 'invaded' by strange lights. They were seen on radar and by commercial aircraft and pursued by military fighters scrambled to investigate. The UFOs even flew over restricted space near the

White House and caused considerable disquiet in the US government.

Churchill's memo shows he was puzzled by the lack of concern coming out of Washington – and urged his Air Minister to provide the PM with something more to base judgement upon. Cochrane reacted by sending a senior Air Ministry scientist , Sir Robert Coburn, over to the States to get to the bottom of what flew over the US capital. On return he briefed Cochrane and Churchill that nobody knew for sure what had 'invaded' Washington but that the Americans were reinforcing their UFO investigation team and so determined to find out.

Days after Coburn was back in London the Dishforth sighting occurred and Churchill was convinced he now needed to act. He created a UK investigation unit within the Air Ministry to match the US one operated out of Wright Patterson Air Force Base in Dayton, Ohio. The UK team operated for 57 years before being closed in 2009 as a cost cutting measure.

As Churchill and Cochrane pondered details of this unit Jenny's confidante Noyes was being charged to discover the facts from Dishforth and Topcliffe air bases about what happened during Operation Mainbrace.

Noyes would tell Jenny: '*Cochrane passed me the NATO signals… I referred them down to air staff and asked for a report.*' But nobody in authority wanted to believe anything strange might really be happening. '*I heard people say things like – blimey, so are some of our chaps being taken in by these hallucinations now?' I was really concerned about the blasé thinking behind such an attitude.'*

As time passed Noyes became convinced that the ministry was unduly complacent – confirmed when he was shown top secret film taken from gun cameras aboard RAF jet aircraft sent to chase UFOs when flying over Britain. Sadly, this 1950s film 'disappeared' from the files before it ever reached the 30 year date allowing public release. But Noyes told Jenny it was '*strange – though not obviously showing any kind of machine*'.

Noyes reported back to Cochrane and Churchill from Yorkshire that Operation Mainbrace had been swamped by UFO sightings during that week in September 1952. The case over Dishforth was only the first. Indeed commander of RAF 269 squadron, 31 year old Flight Lieutenant John Kilburn, started his report on what was witnessed with words only a British officer from a bygone age would write:-

'I have the honour to report the following incident....'

The witnesses on that Autumn morning were two flight lieutenants, a flying officer, two sergeants and a Leading Aircraftman. Kilburn's account describes how the UFO initially descended as if it was riding air currents like a falling leaf – before commencing its rapid rotation. The object then responded and changed course when the Meteor jet seemingly became aware of it and 'locked on'. Initially they suspected that they were watching a parachute canopy floating in the wind. But this extraordinary behavior eliminated that theory.

After about 20 seconds watching this incident unfold over Dishforth in perfect visibility the UFO then raced away westward, before moving south eastward with an acceleration that was '*in excess of that of a shooting star*.'

The very next day a US aircraft carrier in the same NATO exercise – the *Franklin D Roosevelt* – encountered another silver spinning top whilst in the North Sea off the Yorkshire coast. Despite Noyes attempting to learn more facts the Americans did not seem keen to pass much back to the UK through him. It was merely reported to Noyes that it 'circled the ship' and that many personnel on board witnessed it. The ship's photographer also took shots of the UFO but these were never released to the Air Ministry investigation or to Noyes despite his requesting to see them.

However, in 1956 the head of the Ohio based US Air Force UFO study (Captain Ed Ruppelt) confirmed the existence of these photos in a memoir, stating they were 'excellent' and that their sequence showed the high speed of the spinning top as it flew away. He added that they looked for a possible weather balloon launched from another ship to explain the event, but found none.

In the 1980s Noyes, despite his high rank in the MoD, was still unaware of some of these details until Jenny Randles told him some 30 years after he had pursued the matter on behalf of Winston Churchill!

Jenny had discovered more data direct from the USA when travelling the country alongside astronomer Dr J Allen Hynek - who served as the US Air Force science adviser throughout the days of the Wright Patterson UFO project – including during the Mainbrace exercise in the UK.

Hynek assessed cases for the US government right up to closure of its UFO project in 1969 and then rallied fellow scientists to the cause. He even teamed up with famous movie producer Steven Spielberg to create the film 'Close Encounters of the Third Kind' which was developed out of a book that Hynek wrote in 1972.

Noyes had by now figured out himself why the Americans had been reluctant to talk to him in 1952 about what happened aboard their ship. This aircraft carrier was the only vessel in the world then fitted with nuclear missiles and its security surpassed even the special relationship with post war Britain.

Twenty four hours after that sighting from the carrier, on 21 September 1952, six RAF planes off the Yorkshire coast observed yet another silver top shape approach them. One Meteor played 'tag' with this object for a while before it seemed to lose interest and streaked away at incredible speed.

After so many events during a NATO exercise it was inevitable that Churchill would agree a British UFO investigation team set up at Whitehall. Ralph Noyes was in at the start and RAF Dishforth had been instrumental in it happening. Wartime hero Winston clearly took UFOs seriously in an age when most people did not.

But as I entered Dishforth for training I had no idea that this MoD UFO investigation team which was set up as a consequence of events right here 30 years earlier would soon become very interested in me!

As a young recruit to the Yorkshire police nothing could have prepared me for what Dishforth was like. The weather was wet with a kind of smog that hung in the air and there was an icy wind that cut right through to the bone. There was a sense of dread that appeared to be circulating amongst the arriving bands of new recruits. No one knew what to expect of the next thirteen weeks, but if the reception was anything to go by, then it would be no walk in the park.

Awaiting my turn in the queue at the reception desk a rather large hand placed itself upon my shoulder.

" *Shouldn't you be in the other queue, miss*?" a very quiet voice whispered in my ear.

Looking puzzled I turned towards the voice and saw a rather large uniformed sergeant with the peak of his cap slashed, so it lay flat on his forehead like a guardsman.

Before I could reply he suddenly screamed at the top of his voice:- " *Get your fucking hair cut you big tart and what's that caterpillar doing on your top lip*".

I did not know whether to laugh or cry, but before I could say anything, I was following him to a chair in the corner where I was sat down in front of a rather jolly man, who cut my hair shorter than on the day of my birth. All this in front of both queues of recruits – men and women - though, happily, the barber did leave my 'tash alone.

Our two story barrack block was divided on each floor into halves with the wash rooms and toilets in the middle. That was a bit of an eye opener for me, too. I was on the top floor sharing with thirteen other lads and our beds were laid out down both sides of the room with a small set of drawers and an even smaller wardrobe by the side of each. In the middle of the room were two sets of tables pushed together to form a large square.

I remember that room as stark and sparse – devoid of any form of home comfort, but this was an RAF camp and I suppose this is what military personnel were expected to put up with, so we had to get on with it too.

The following morning was our first parade and we were addressed by the camp commander, a chief superintendent by rank. There were about 250 of us at the front of the parade square, with as many again at the back. Those other recruits had already done the first six weeks of their training and it showed when they all marched off in unison.

After the parade we were put into groups, all the lads from the dorm were added to my group and we were joined by six female officers and marched off by those who were to become our class sergeants for the full thirteen weeks.

After an introductory lecture, I discovered that I was the oldest amongst the new arrivals - in fact one of the oldest on the course – even though I was just twenty eight years old !

I was made the 'right hand marker' - a sort of lance corporal - and wore a red insignia round the shoulder of the right arm. My job was to look after discipline in the class and dormitory and march our group around the camp to and from lessons and anywhere else that we had to go.

It was my first taste of power!

The weeks dragged by, full of lectures and physical training and learning how to march in formation. But at the end of each week came the dreaded exams - which you could only fail twice.

If you failed once then you had to spend a lot of time at the intensive study department before continuing, but if you failed again, it was goodnight sweetheart and you were on your way home.

Quite a lot of those around me failed, including a couple in our class. Fortunately, I was averaging about eighty five percent pass mark for the weekly exams and had settled down into the strict regime. Then one night, so late that it was actually already early morning, I thought I felt the bed move around me but I was so tired from a very heavy day of physical training and the odd pint that I had consumed afterwards that I decided against worrying too much. So I just rolled over and went back into a deep sleep - until a funny feeling came over me that was niggling in my mind that maybe something really was not right.

Slowly I pulled the covers down and peered over the top of them and found that I was not in the barracks any more. In fact I was in the middle of the parade square and it was freezing cold.

A quick glance round and thankfully no-one was out there at this deathly hour and I ran back to the dormitory to find everyone asleep. Switching on the lights did the trick and after a bloody good laugh and not a little piss taking from the lads they helped me get the bed back up the stairs and into the room.

What I did not know and would not find out until the end of the course, at the formal black tie dinner dance, was that someone had taken some photographs of my 'abduction' and had had them blown up and they were plastered all over the walls of the officers mess.

I made some good friends on that course and we helped each other out in different ways. One lad in our dorm was an ex Paratrooper and he showed us all how to bull your boots up to make them shine like diamond. He also taught us how to march.

You might think that marching was quite easy - just put one leg in front of the other and you are away. But you will be amazed how many people cannot do such a simple thing. The problems start when you swing your arms in the opposite direction to your legs. Try it, if you think it sounds a doddle! Just to watch grown men endeavoring to move their arms and legs in an approximation of perfect harmony was funny. In reality they looked like robots and no matter how hard they tried many could not overcome this problem.

Dave would spend hours attempting to teach them to do this right and he was very successful in most cases. He was actually forming a bonding relationship with these men – the kind of comradeship that would stay with you throughout your career in the police.

Such friendships developed over my thirteen weeks at Dishforth and it taught us how to work as a team and look after one another's back. This would prove invaluable in future when things began to get very ugly within the force. You need your mates at times like that.

However, the events heading my way would stretch even that bond of kinship close to breaking point.

At last came the passing out parade and it was special – involving formation marching with intricate moves. As right marker I had to bellow out '*eyes right'* and salute the officers then on parade.

I was so proud as my family and friends had all come to watch this final spectacle.

Returning to Wakefield after those tiring weeks, was a piece of cake by comparison. The drill sergeant turned out to be a real gent and he told me that he was pleased that no officer from my small section had failed that year.

Yes - all of my charges had passed out and as a thank you for getting us this far we presented our 'sarge' with a silver tankard.

As for the survivors - we were now officially ready to face the world.

We were about to become police officers.

CHAPTER TWO

On the beat....at last!

The next week at Wakefield passed very quickly as I eagerly awaited my first posting from the personnel department. When it arrived it was great news - I was assigned to Halifax division and stationed at Todmorden.

I was coming home.

But just how would I cope with working as a police officer in the town where I had grown up. And how would my old friends react if I had to speak with them in an official capacity? Pretty soon I was going to find out.

For hopefully understandable reasons, I will change the names of certain parties in this chapter to spare their embarrassment and, on occasion, legal discretion demands it whilst discussing 'cases' on the beat.

Those first tours of duty were with PC Lindsay, who acted as my tutor constable. He was well liked as a copper, not only within the job but outside in the wider community where he commanded respect. Coming as he did from the old school of policing - no nonsense, but fair – he would rather tell you off than book you for a minor offence and also had a way of calming a potentially violent situation with his laid back approach.

Because of his reputation for these things I was very grateful to be guided by him. He taught me how to respect other people, by treating and speaking to them as you would expect to be spoken to and treated yourself.

Of course, he also had to steer me through those first weeks and show me how to do the job that I had trained for – such as dealing with the procedure required when booking people for minor offences. Doing that in the real world was quite different from the way we learned in training and a lot harder – though after a while you got used to it.

I worried that my social life would change in the face of this new role in the community. To some extent it did - friends seemed more distant and conversations suddenly stopped or changed subject when I appeared.

Then came my first time at court where a case that I had policed was to be heard. The guy was pleading guilty to a minor road traffic offence, but I had to be there just in case he changed his mind at the last minute. I need not have worried as when the matter came around he did plead guilty. However, despite this and instead of the prosecuting inspector reading the facts and simply reporting my statement to the magistrates, he thought it would be a good idea for me to give evidence from the witness box.

I was horrified.

I can still remember him saying to the magistrates: *"PC Godfrey, the officer in this case, is here in court today and has never given evidence before. I think it will be a good opportunity for him to do so now."*

Stepping into the box and swearing the oath and speaking my name, I could feel my heart trying to burst out of my chest as it was beating so fast. Then the chairman asked me if I was one of the Godfreys that used to live at the chip shop on Brook Street, and, after confirming that I was, he went on to ask how my parents were and whether they still lived on the Isle of Wight.

The look on the face of the solicitors that were in court acting for other defendants due to appear later that day was a picture. They must have wondered what was going on here, watching magistrates being so friendly with the police and almost treating one another like long lost friends. I imagine that they were concerned about how they could properly challenge any evidence given by police if the magistrates were all pals with them?

That reasonable concern was unfounded, of course, because I can assure you, they never showed favour to myself or fellow officers and treated each case fairly. Still it was a delight to see those lawyer's faces nonetheless.

I was glad for that chance to give evidence before magistrates so early in my career as I could now operate without constant apprehension over what it would be like. It was something that all coppers must get used to and the sooner that you break your duck the faster the nerves disappear and you can just get on with the job.

Eventually the station was happy to allow me to

police on my own and I could put into practice all of the experience and expertise that PC Lindsay had taught me. This was already paying dividends.

The next big milestone that I saw looming with dread would be my first case of a sudden death. All police officers will confront one sooner or later and knowing that I would have to sit in on my first post mortem at the mortuary right after attending such a tragic situation did rather play on my mind in the weeks before it happened.

I was told all sorts of myths by fellow officers on what went on at the mortuary so I replied bravely how I had seen many dead bodies when working in the prison service. That was completely untrue, but the kind of macho thing that you say when young to bluff your way through any scary situation. I was just hoping to convince my colleagues that I was prepared.

If only it were that simple.

It was about half six in the morning, having just come on duty, when I was informed that a local doctor had reported a sudden death. It was not considered to be suspicious, but he could not legally issue a death certificate without having recently seen the deceased to attest to their state of health. The law required this safeguard when faced by an as yet unexplained demise.

Nevertheless, I was assured, this case was considered to be a tragic heart attack without suspicious circumstances. So I went to the house and took details from the family and arranged for the deceased to be removed to the mortuary.

I could not touch the body. This was actually the first time I had even seen one, although I kept that news to myself, of course.

Jeff - the officer working the front desk and with years of experience – had told me that he would come with me to the post mortem and privately I was very relieved to be offered his support. I could not imagine doing this first time all on my own.

The morning seemed to drag by and I could not eat breakfast knowing what I was about to witness. Then – to my horror - Jeff came into the mess room and apologised as he had to go out on another call.

What was I going to do now? I was being sent to face a dead body alone.

One of the lads drove me to Hebden Bridge Police station to pick up the keys for the mortuary. Here I first met PC Jack Brierley and we would become very close friends. Our paths, both within the job and away from work, would cross on many further occasions. Even today, after all these years, we remain best mates – but more of Jack later.

Hopefully most of you have never had the sad experience of being inside a mortuary - but the first thing that overpowers you is this kind of sickly smell which is hard to describe, yet it sticks to your clothing for hours. I was taken aback by this unexpected sensation, but determined not to let anyone know.

The room itself was small with white tiles on the walls and two long marble slabs each having a large plug hole at one end. I felt cold knowing that there – laid out in the middle of the room - was a body covered in a white sheet - the subject of my case.

Jack, my one companion, could see I was not well:-

"*First time is it son*?" he said gently.

I replied that it was.

"*Not to worry...There is only one way that you will ever get used to being around dead bodies and that is to shake hands with one.*"

I momentarily froze. What could he possibly mean?

"*Come on lad,*" he added, sensing my surprise.

I was taken aback at this bizarre suggestion, but was lead toward the body under the sheet. My colleague pulled the covers back a little and picked up the arm of the deceased for me to grip hold and shake its hand.

Steeling myself against inner horrors I took a deep breath and reached out. If he thinks it will help, I whispered to myself.

As soon as I carefully took hold of the hand that was underneath the sheet, the palm that I was touching wriggled back into life. The fingers grasped me very hard and the dead body sat bolt upright.

I do not mind telling you that I screamed and tried to run out of the room. But I could not escape – because this *dead man* had a powerful grip.

Then I saw the wristwatch he was wearing and felt the warmth of his hand trickle through to my senses. The truth dawned that this was not a dead body at all but a perfectly healthy one.

It was a joke – an initiation of sorts for a green copper. As Jack grinned back at me from ear to ear I could have killed him.

The post mortem on the real deceased gentleman went ahead alongside the pathologist. And - yes - I did shake hands with the unfortunate victim as Jack suggested that I should. Surprisingly it did work and having to deal with dead bodies never worried me again after enduring this scary 'rite of passage'.

A few years later I was to be very grateful for that initiation ceremony, because it was to be another dead body that I would confront one wet afternoon which would change my destiny.

His name was Zygmund Jan Adamski and he would become one of the most baffling cases in the history of Yorkshire sudden deaths.

But we shall reach that tragic story soon enough.

My first couple of years as a copper at Todmorden went very well. I had settled in and was getting good work appraisals from the officers above me and passing several exams on the way.

The required two year probationary period was nearing its end and that would be a great relief for me. If I could jump that final hurdle then I would become a fully-fledged police constable.

Those early years on the job tested me in many ways. Especially on one day when I had to deal with a fatal road accident that was caused by a driver who had been drinking. Sadly, the man who caused this tragedy was a good friend of mine whom I had known since school. In the 1960s we had hung around together as teens in a gang of Rocker mates. We dressed in leather jackets and rode our motor bikes like many a youth of that decade.

There were some good scraps in those days – usually with lads from nearby towns - and we sorted out some local Mods from time to time. Perhaps looking back this was not model behavior for a budding copper but we are all young and foolish once and everyone has to grow up.

Even so in those days you could have put a year's wages on my ending up on the other side of this sort of fracas. But as a policeman it was now me charged with bringing order rather than creating this sort of chaos.

On one of those riotous nights of my youth during a party at my parent's house on Brook Street my mate and I decided that it would be a good idea to paint my car. It was definitely not wise under the circumstances!

That car was an old Ford Zodiac and my pal and I were drunk out of our heads and had just had a race, stark naked, toward a drink machine that was situated on the corner of the market building and bus station. To prove that you had succeeded you had to run back with a hot drink. It was a bloody good laugh.

After these exertions I had remembered that my dad had some old tins of blue gloss paint. So we decided to use these and took my car and parked it under the arch at the top of Hall Street near Sunnyside, just in case it rained. Here we would keep the vehicle dry as we set about painting the old dear.

Well the following day after we had all sobered up we went to see how our creation was looking. Unfortunately it was covered in dead midges stuck fast to the drying paint, looking rather like a woolen blanket. It was not exactly the work of art we had been aiming to achieve. I do not remember what I did with that old car – I suspect I had to scrap it.

Now years after these harmless escapades I faced the much more sobering prospect of having to deal with my old mate in my capacity as a police officer and after he had just caused someone's death by driving whilst apparently drunk.

I could not let my feelings show, either to him or anybody else. He knew what he had done was terribly wrong and how hard it was for me to be there. But he now had to live with his conscience and account for his actions on that day for the rest of his life. He would never really get over what he had done, yet we remained good friends until his untimely death some years later.

My early years as a police officer did have low moments such as these amidst the mundane things that fill up most of your time. But all was going well until the arrival at the station of an ex-CID officer who had just been promoted to sergeant and assigned onto our shift.

Like all those before him, including newly appointed inspectors, he believed that he was going to change the world and stop the plague of after time drinking. Todmorden had evolved a bit of a reputation for such a problem. But I did not hold out much hope for him surviving too long at Tod given his determination to succeed in this quest. This activity was a tradition that had gone on for as long as anyone could remember in the town's hostelries.

In fact one long serving inspector encouraged it, saying that he would rather have a peaceful town centre late at night when people finally left the pub to head home. But if you made them all go together in one crowd bang on closing time their mood was often different. Everybody congregated out on the streets at the same moment and trouble easily followed. As a result twice as many bobbies were needed to deal with strictly enforcing the law.

How right he was. But that did not stop some newly promoted sergeants and inspectors with what they thought of as modern methods from trying to enforce a curfew. They quickly discovered that there were well known ways to make their clean-up efforts just a little bit harder and the natives were experts at them all.

On one occasion this newly arrived sergeant, who had kept to himself which pub he intended to raid that night in case it got back to the landlord, asked me and some other officers to meet him near to his selected target. He had been watching it for quite a while and was convinced it was flouting the law after closing time and so we were ordered to go in and stop that practice.

The sergeant marched in with us and instructed the landlord that it was after hours for serving beer and he must ask his drinkers to leave now.

To which the man behind the bar gave a good old Yorkshire reply that I still laugh at today:-

"It's taken me all neet to get the buggers in and I'm not going to tell them to leave now".

So he carried on serving.

The sergeant looked at his officers and told us to take the name and address of everyone present and report them for drinking after time. Once we were back at the police station we found him walking around like a young cock loose in a shed of chickens, full of himself.

"Well lads how many did you report?" He asked us chirpily.

I told him my list and how I had recorded a certain *Mr Mickey Mouse* of this parish, and a *Mr Elvis Presley* – quite an unusual name for a Yorkshire lad, I added. He looked at me thunderstruck but all his other officers reported similar – obviously fallacious - identities.

Of course, the sergeant went mad. No, actually, he glared at us incandescent with rage and, for some reason, did not seem to see the funny side like we all did. It takes all sorts, I suppose.

Unfortunately for me this innocuous incident was a turning point and this sergeant started to make the final few weeks of my probationary period harder than they should have been. It all culminated in a dramatic event.

I was out on patrol in one of the panda cars and enjoying a quiet moment eating a Chinese takeaway. This was not unusual when working late. I had parked up on what is now the site of the Morrisons Supermarket delivery area, but back then it was still Waterside Mill which was occupied by a plastics company. They famously manufactured a so called 'house of the future' – called 'Futuro' – a modular dome which looked like something out of the cartoon series The Jetsons and had a bit of a flying saucer shape to it. That house would figure in my story years later when it apparently grew wings and gave nocturnal pleasure flights over Tod – if you believe some of the more imaginative UFO skeptics!

But on that night in my late 1970s patrol car - rather like the one I am standing next to in this photo from that time - I was not thinking about any of this. Just my dinner.

Little else was going on around town at the time except for me eating my chicken chow mein. But after reaching the end of the meal I suddenly heard an almighty roar of an engine and the screeching of tyres. Within seconds this car went screaming past the entrance to where I was parked not displaying any lights.

I threw the Chinese takeaway onto the passenger

seat and drove off in pursuit with my blue lights flashing. After pursuing the offender towards Rochdale in a high speed chase I managed to make him stop near to the 'Bird in T'hand' pub. Here I discovered that the driver was a young man in his twenties who got out after I had forced him to a halt and I slowly walked over to speak to him.

I enquired officiously:-

"Do you always drive the car at night without lights?"

He just smirked back at me and pointed to my patrol car saying:-

"Do you?"

I glanced back at my vehicle and – oh dear - he was right. Only the police sign and the blue flashing lights were on. Not my headlights!

Luckily I had the last laugh - his cocky attitude made sure of that. I could smell on his breath that he had been drinking and knew that I had to 'bag' him.

This was the nickname for the old fashioned breathalyser kit used in the seventies. It came in a square green plastic box and on the inside was a row of small glass phials which had a nipple at each end and a line across the middle. The contraption was filled with crystals that would turn green when alcohol was introduced via the breath of the user. A plastic bag had to be attached to one end for the driver's breath to enter, hence the term 'bagged'.

Having got the young man safely seated in the patrol car and the breath kit assembled I went through the expected legal jargon of requesting him to provide a specimen of breath and instructed him on how to do that as required by law. The chap took a deep breath and blew into the kit but without any success inflating the bag. I warned him to try harder and that to fail to provide a specimen would lead to his immediate arrest. Then after appearing to go blue in the face whilst blowing as much as he could but still without being able to inflate the bag I booked him and took him back to the station.

All the while the young man was protesting his innocence as we drove back to town. He continued these protestations to my duty sergeant once we had arrived. So I showed the kit to the officer and explained what had happened. The young man was 'booked in' as a prisoner and offered a second chance to supply a specimen as allowed by law. He quickly accepted.

I started to dismantle the breath kit and when I removed the bag and mouthpiece I noticed that I had forgotten to break the nipples off the ends of the phial preventing any chemical reaction. I had accidentally made the kit impossible for the man to use and he might well have gone free as a consequence of my mistake.

A wry smile spread across my face as I conveniently dropped the remains into the waste basket at the side of my desk and assembled a new kit – this time remembering to break the nipples off and ensure that the young man had no trouble inflating the bag now. Sadly for him the crystals turned bright green right away and were far over the middle line. The test was positive.

Later, after giving a sample of blood to the duty doctor our speedster was proven well over the legal limit and got a 12 month ban and a hefty fine.

I did wonder what that sergeant would have done had he been aware of my cock-up whilst assembling the first bag. My probationary period was nearing its end and he was looking for an excuse to have a go at me. I never gave him that chance and happily justice was served and a dangerous driver taken off our streets.

Another day I was out on foot patrol in the town centre having my usual walk around the market stalls and speaking to the traders and shoppers to make sure that all was well. Then somebody came up to me and informed me that there was a man nearby who appeared to be drunk and acting up outside the post office on Brook Street.

I made my way there to check things out and as I approached I could hear the man shouting and swearing at people who were trying to enter the building. He was clearly causing distress to customers and when he saw me arrive took up a fighting pose and became aggressive in his behavior towards me.

As calmly as I could I told him to settle down and behave himself, but to no avail. He just kept shouting:-

"Come on ya bastard - I'll have you - fucking coppers!"

After a few minutes of trying to cool the situation down I called for back-up, but seized a momentary opportunity that gave chance to restrain him. He had taken his eyes off me and was shouting angrily at a rapidly gathering crowd intrigued by his antics. They were now clearly at risk of physical harm.

I subdued him with a defensive movement that we were taught during training at Dishforth for situations just like this and which took his feet from under him. When he was on the ground I managed to handcuff him to the delight of the crowd who had become concerned for their safety by this point.

The poor chap screamed that I had 'assaulted' him when we arrived back at the police station and that sergeant seemed to take heart at this thought and go out of his way to try to get me up on a charge instead of the man I had just arrested. This was all terribly upsetting, but, thankfully, he faced a local public who just told him that my actions were proportional and necessary to protect them from harm. And so he did not pursue his efforts any further.

However, needless to say my last appraisal from that sergeant was not good. I did not recognize myself in the things that he was writing about. Happily it made no difference and I sailed through despite his efforts.

So now it was official and I had become a fully-fledged police constable, but one who would remember this little man and his ways.

There is a saying around Yorkshire that you should do unto others as they have done unto you - but make sure that you do it better.

That is exactly what I would do with this particular person – as you will find out later.

Unfortunately it was not long after finishing my probation that I faced a nightmare that would have a profound impact on my life both in the job and, more importantly, at home. This happened on 23rd October 1977 – a date forever etched into my mind.

We were on night duty and it had been raining hard and so I was soaked after being on foot patrol across the town centre for the first half of the evening dealing with its usual routine of drunks and disorderly behaviour.

Nothing had been serious enough to warrant an arrest, but at last I was on my way back to the station for a well-earned cup of tea, when a radio message came through that three youths had badly assaulted an inspector in his office at the bus station. Would I go over and check things out.

After getting a description and a name for one of the youths who had been recognized by a witness I made a search of the area looking for the perpetrators. It proved negative so I returned back to the station where I still had another round of duty.

The second part of my shift was as the driver of one of the two patrol cars, my call sign being *Alpha Bravo Three*. It was whilst out in that vehicle that I came across the three youths who had been involved in the assault. By chance they were very near to our police station and had suddenly appeared from one of the darkened back streets before fleeing when they saw my panda car.

It looked as if they had been hiding out in one of their mate's houses and had kept themselves well out of sight for the past few hours. So, after radioing in my sighting of them, I caught up with the suspects and got out of the car to have a word.

At the same time I spotted several of my fellow officers running down the street from the station towards me to provide back up to what was a hazardous arrest of potentially dangerous persons. But I could not wait for help or the suspect would escape, so I attempted to arrest the one that had been named by the witness. He was determined not to come quietly and a struggle ensued.

Suddenly, I felt an awful searing pain in my groin. I recoiled backwards doubled up in agony.

The rest of the lads arrived soon after having witnessed the attack as they closed in. Now they grabbed hold of the writhing suspect. The youth was going berserk as the other two ran off and left him. It took four of us to carry this screaming and struggling maniac back to the station and all the time I was in terrible pain and felt like I wanted to be sick.

My suffering was indescribable and to make matters worse the youth took hold of my thumb in the jaws of his mouth and tried to bite it off and cut so deep that he nearly succeeded as blood spurted everywhere.

By the time we got him into the station he was still fighting with the others as I collapsed onto the floor no longer able to control the pain.

Eventually he was locked away inside a cell and an ambulance was called. But by now I could not even breathe because of the extent of the stabbing sensations in my groin. Before I knew what was happening I was falling down and losing consciousness, the pain getting worse and the swelling in my groin growing by the minute. One of the lads undid my belt and trousers in an attempt to ease the swelling that was already evident in my nether regions and I can just vaguely remember the ambulance crew arriving.

There was an audible gasp from the room when the medics finally got my trousers and underpants down. My left testicle had swollen to the size of an Easter egg and there was no sign of the right one at all. The ambulance men told my colleagues that they believed that it had been kicked so hard it had gone back inside of me, a diagnosis later confirmed in hospital.

They stemmed the blood flow from my thumb and then quickly put me into the ambulance and we made a trip with blue lights flashing all the way to hospital. I remember little of this journey as I was drifting in and out of consciousness, but I do recall seeing Jack in the ambulance as he, too, had been assaulted by my assailant and was in pain from his injuries.

On arrival at the accident and emergency department I was given large doses of morphine before being transferred to Burnley General Hospital. For the next few days I was on a drip that sent much needed pain killers coursing through my system but slowly I was coming to terms with what had happened to me in just a few moments.

At least when one of our Inspectors and a sergeant came to the ward to see me I was able to have a bit of a laugh – even though it hurt like hell to do so. I was sat up in bed with my legs being kept apart by a plastic splint and what was left of my crown jewels were being supported on top of it in a bed of cotton wool and lint like a birds nest.

When they asked me how I was feeling, I threw back the covers and showed them this X rated sight – and said:-

'How do you think?'

The officers turned away and looked as if they were about to throw up.

I can laugh now at the memory of that night, but then, if I coughed, never mind laughed, my body was overcome by intense waves of agony.

A week went by before the swelling had gone down sufficiently for an examination by the consultant, who was a large Scottish gentleman who smoked a pipe on the ward. No clap trap then about second hand smoke being radio-active to others.

The consultant could only inform me that it would be a long time before he could say what the extent of the damage was going to be. But, he added, ensuring that I understood that it was very serious – that I must prepare myself for the worst outcome.

The left testicle would need micro surgery as it had split open and required reconstruction. That was – however - the best case scenario as he might have to remove it completely once they took a closer look inside.

As for my right testicle - that had gone into my stomach and he hoped it would come back down on its own, but only time would tell if that would happen or if it would ever function again even if it did. He might have to remove that one too.

Naturally this all left me devastated. The pain was bad enough, but now I had to face the real prospect I might lose both testicles at such a young age.

I had many visitors during the weeks that followed and sometimes it was hard to put on a brave face. Explaining to loved ones what might happen was something I could not yet think about, so I just pretended that everything was fine and I would soon be home.

The operation on the left testicle was a success and, thank goodness, it did not need to be removed. But until the right one decided to return into the world, I would not know if I would lead a normal life again.

Not all was doom and gloom during that anxious wait – though - because one night the matron was making her rounds and all the nurses were running around like chickens clucking in her wake. She was checking each patient and chatting to them as she moved around the ward. When she got to my bed, I was having a smoke and listening to the hospital radio, she said to me:

"Ah, hello - and how are you today, Mr Oddball?"

I nearly choked at these words and the nurses nearby had to struggle in order to keep a straight face.

One of my visitors had changed the name on the medical board at the bottom of the bed from Godfrey to Oddball!

I think I replied something like my oddball "*was feeling very lonely*" and matron looked rather puzzled at this curious reply. At least until I had explained about my situation 'down below'. Then she could not stop laughing. Though I never found out which of my visitors quietly changed the name, on the board I certainly have my suspicions!

Eventually I was released home again and a long road to recovery began. This would be far from easy, and I was scared that my family might suffer through my bouts of depression and mood swings as I fretted about the future.

During those weeks at home I started drinking and could get quite verbally angry and say some awful things that I came to regret. I think my children suffered as I would shout at them for no reason and apologise for everything the following day when I had sobered up.

This all became a vicious circle from which I was unable to escape.

So it was a relief when one of the Inspectors came round to our house and offered me the front desk job at the station on regular shifts. This was a light duty out of the firing line on the beat but I jumped at the chance to escape the house and go back to doing something useful. Frankly, it made me feel like a man again which was very important in that period.

It was now 1979 and I had been working the front desk for about 6 months as a long hot summer sweltered outside. Being stuck inside the station for hours on end was beginning to frustrate me.

By then we had gone through an influx of young probationers, both male and female, who had been posted to Todmorden and most of them had moved into the police flats just across the road from the station. Each shift was allocated some of these newbies and we had a nice lad who we nicked named 'Rosy' after a character from a police TV show on at that time.

One sunny Sunday 'Rosy' had been out on foot patrol and came back into the station for a brew which saw him pass by me to go to do this. I asked him whilst in the kitchen to make one for me and another for the sergeant - then in his office doing some paperwork.

At the time I was distracted being on the phone taking a call when this figure suddenly loomed behind me and, as I looked over my shoulder cautiously, was shocked to see a rather large gentleman dressed in green cord trousers and wearing a woolly jumper.

I asked him who he was and why he was at the station desk and pointed out the 'Private' sign on the front desk door. His reply stunned me:-

"*I could be a terrorist for all you seem to care if you only have the security of an unlocked door to prevent an attack. Even the dustbin man could get in here*!

'What on Earth!!' – I thought to myself - who was this cheeky sod.

The most likely option was that he might be a patient from Stansfield View Hospital which then looked after people with mental health problems. We used to get them wandering into the station from time to time and we would contact the hospital and return these troubled individuals or look after them until a member of staff could take them back to the safety of their residence. They never caused us problems and were usually just inquisitive about what was going on around them.

But these thoughts were jolted when this gentleman announced that he was actually an ACC - Assistant Chief Constable - and gave his name. So following proper procedure I asked the ACC for his warrant card to confirm his identity - which unfortunately he said that he had not got with him.

By now I was even more convinced that he was another patient who had meandered over from the hospital. So I asked him to go and sit down in one of our detention rooms whilst I 'got help'. By which I really meant that I would phone the mental hospital to come and collect him.

So I took the poor man gently by the arm to lead him off and he shrugged and then just pushed me very firmly away. I knew this was not heading towards a good situation and a struggle soon followed and I shouted to fellow officers to render assistance.

My sergeant was first to respond - rushing out of his office to find the poor 'deluded' man shouting at me and wriggling to escape. Together the 'sarge' and I both managed to get the patient into the detention room in the hope of calming him down until a nurse could arrive.

The man was kicking out with his feet as we took him there and even made a swing at us both with his fist which caught the sergeant on his shoulder. He reacted in self defence and struck a straight jab onto the poor man's chin as we forced him into the room and together just about managed to lock the door.

'Rosy' had by now dashed out of the kitchen and was asking what all the commotion was about. Then he looked into the detention room through the small glass window to see the 'inmate' that we had successfully subdued and the young PC promptly saluted the man!

Of course, I assumed that this new copper was just playing a joke on us and told him to not be silly but he insisted that we had got it terribly wrong.

'That man is a senior officer,' he spluttered. *'I have seen him at headquarters when he gave us probationers a lecture before we got sent off on our postings'*.

At this news I started to feel uneasy and we all sat down with our brew and I began to ask myself if I had just made one heck of a mistake.

Remembering that there was a poster in the sergeants office with pictures of all the different chief officers on it we both went to look at this with trepidation growing. Sure enough there he was. The same man I had just bundled into the detention room and locked up was staring right back from the poster and *was* indeed an Assistant Chief Constable.

"Okay, night all - I'm off" said the sergeant as he headed for the door." *It's your problem now, I was never here – understood!"* he added as he rapidly departed.

'Rosy' decided it was a good idea for him to head out on patrol and used the back door to make his own swift 'escape'. That left me with the task of trying to work out how to get out of this bloody great mess.

Actually I started to chuckle to myself as this was all like a plot out of the popular Yorkshire sitcom 'Last of the Summer wine' where daft situations like this were invented in the lives of the local folk and bobbies around the nearby small town of Holmfirth. Except this was not a sit com. It was very real.

Of course, I should not have been giggling given this tricky predicament but I just could not stop, probably because I had no idea what else to do.

Taking a deep breath I opened the detention room door and said: "*Who was it that you claimed to be, sir – the Chief Constable?*"

He was not amused, but informed me that his warrant card was in his coat pocket which was outside with his wife currently waiting for him in their car.

"*Um, okay then, sir, I will go and check*," I replied, attempting to sound both fair and efficient whilst under full control of things.

His wife was indeed outside in the car and by now rather upset. She asked me to tell her husband to hurry up as the plants they had just bought at Gordon Riggs needed to be taken home and watered before they wilted.

"*I'll tell him that, madam*", I responded as matter of factly as I could.

Of course, I then released the ACC from his confinement and – after he had taken my name and collar number – was advised rather curtly that he would be speaking to the Chief Superintendent about this incident and off he went.

‘*Bloody Hell’* I said to myself, I can see a transfer to Leeds and walking between two lamp posts for the rest of my career after this.

A couple of hours passed as I sat there alone with a gathering sense of doom. Then ‘you know who’ was on the phone: “ *Yes sir… I did sir…Yes sir… That’s right sir…Ten o’clock Sir… Wednesday …Your office…Yes sir’* - was about the entire gist of my side of the conversation with the chief super.

It was followed rapidly by ‘*Shit! Shit! Shit*!’ under my breath to myself as I put the phone down.

It was not too long before the story of this incident was all over the force and talked about in every station. They say that the police grapevine travels at twice the speed of light which was not wrong on this occasion.

For the next couple of days every time I answered the internal phone line the voice on the other end would come out with some witty remark like:

‘*This is the chief constable here - could I speak to the jailer*’

I knew it was just my colleagues joshing about and took it in good spirit.

But then I answered one last occasion and the voice said: "*Chief Superintendent here .... could you put me through to the Inspectors office*".

Having had enough I quickly replied : -

"*Look just F*** Off I have now had enough of this bullshit from all you lot...*"

Before I could even finish the sentence it became all too obvious that on this occasion it was not a trick and really *was* the Chief Superintendent!

The following Wednesday arrived and I found myself outside the Chief Super's office all dressed in my best uniform and with my boots the most highly polished I could get them to be.

To say that I was nervous would be putting it mildly. I was really worried about how far they were going to transfer me across the county. My only glimmer of comfort was that I knew that if they were charging me with assault on the ACC then I would already be in front of the chief constable facing arrest, so I just I wanted to know the extent of my punishment and get it over with.

All over the force they were having sweepstakes to see who could guess the number of miles that I was about to be transferred away from Tod. Can you believe that from some of my mates...though I did not blame them and even had a little bet on myself!

But in the end nobody won because I just got reprimanded for being overly zealous with my restraint. Apparently the ACC had decided on the hoof to try out the security at Todmorden station and said that he left his warrant card in his car on purpose and because I had asked to see it I had done the right thing. Had I simply believed him without proof then I would have been in serious trouble. The assistant chief's main complaint was that the counter door should have been locked!

This story went down in police training history and was later used to teach new recruits exactly why it was essential to always carry your warrant card and why police officers must always check the ID of others to get proof of whatever they say.

A few weeks after this episode and 'Rosy' was by now getting on very well at his posting in Todmorden . He loved the job and felt happy in the local community as well and had even joined the local cricket club, turning out for them on a regular basis when his shifts would allow.

I liked 'Rosy', he was a bit quiet and not really the temperament of what you would expect of a policeman back in those days. He just got on with the job without fuss and sometimes kept himself to himself.

Then one day, whilst we were on an early shift from 6am to 2pm, the phone rang and it was the lollypop lady who helped children to cross the road outside the nearby school. She was phoning in to say she was unwell that day and could we send cover for her, which we usually did if manpower and other duties allowed.

Immediately a little thought came into my head and a broad smile appeared right across my face as it developed.

'Rosy' came into the station for his meal break at about 8.30am and I told him he must go and do the school crossing, which surprisingly he had never done before. So off he went upstairs to the locker room and reappeared with his white gloves and was just about to go out of the front door when I said:

"Haven't you forgotten something?"

I pointed to the large 'STOP' sign that would be held up to prevent traffic or children crossing at the wrong moment. He gave me a funny look but picked it up and trooped off on his way. I could not stop laughing as he waddled off.

Rosy was a little bit upset when he returned to the station for me sending him on this 'mission', but we had many a laugh about it afterward. Indeed I was sad to hear some months after that incident that 'Rosy' chose to leave the job and move to Burnley. I still wonder what happened to him.

It was hard stuck in the station all the time just answering the phone and manning the enquiry desk. This was not why I had joined the force, so I asked if I could go back to normal duties, even though medical advice about my still unresolved injuries following the assault was that I should carry on with light duties or risk further potentially permanent complications.

Happily my request was granted and I could not wait to get back out onto the streets. And once in the 'real world' I soon returned to my normal self. Sadly at home life was not so good and became even more strained. My injuries even all this time later remained severe and compromised relationships to the point of real strain.

All of this turned me into something of a Jekyll and Hyde character, nice as pie one minute and a right so and so the next.

Then one evening whilst I was having a soothing bath I suddenly felt a strange sensation together with a lot of pain down below. I coughed and as I did so my right testicle returned from its exile and took up residence in my nether regions. What a weird sensation that was, but it came as a massive relief as it had seemed for so long like I might be incapacitated for life.

I looked down and for the first time I felt normal in that area again. I could not wait to see the consultant and quickly made an appointment. To my delight after a thorough examination he informed me that the still blackened testicle should recover to a more normal colour and hopefully settle back into its proper position. For now it had lodged itself at the top of my groin.

Alas it never did move, so I had to undergo yet another operation to correct this as best as they could. It was some months after that surgery before things really started to get back to normal, in most senses of the word.

Life back at the nick in the meantime carried on as usual and I had some good laughs with the rest of the lads. Until one day we had another new inspector who proved to be like no other. I can only describe him as akin to the character portrayed on TV by the late Warren Clarke, Superintendent Andy Dalziel, in the popular long running Dalziel and Pascoe detective series.

Like the Pennine copper in that TV drama our inspector was a rather portly man, barrel bodied and with a gruff and broad Yorkshire accent. He also had a habit of scratching his crotch all the time.

My first encounter with him came as we paraded for duty prior to going out on the beat. It was at this point that the shift would be informed about what had been going on during the previous twenty-four hours and any relevant crime reports or updates were provided. We were all stood in a line and he was walking back and forth staring hard into the eyes of those he passed.

Then he said in a dramatic voice:

"I am the wind and you are the grass, when I blow you will bend, do we understand one another?' Adding ominously – *'I will not put up with your ways!"*

A reference to how policing in Tod was done.

Before too long he changed his tune. This was largely because nobody would speak to him until he came around and he was getting cold shouldered. He even had to bring his own refreshments because we declined to let him join our tea fund.

It was one particular event that would bring him round to our quiet but efficient way of policing that suited a small town such as ours.

Our new governor had instructed us all to increase the station's conviction rate in order to make the annual crime statistics look better.

As a result of this edict you would not believe how many car owners came into the station to complain demanding to see the inspector with a new way of doing things and responsible for the consequences.

Of course, our boss was not a 'happy chappy' to see his efforts misfire but it was an unfortunate set of circumstances shall we say.

We had all gone out during a night shift and placed 'Fixed Penalty Notice Tickets' onto hundreds of cars in an attempt to follow his instructions to the letter.

These owners were guilty of very minor misdemeanours, such as parking within 15 yards of a junction without lights or facing the wrong way round. Usually in these circumstances we would have issued a warning and no more - if we had bothered about this small matter at all.

Nevertheless they were all technically offences and we had been ordered to enforce the law by our leader and every one of them carried a fixed penalty fine. As a result the blitz gave the inspector his desired rise in the conviction rates.

The response of the public was exactly what we knew that it would be because the price for such a strict approach had been a simmering resentment amongst the locals. Needless to say the inspector soon saw why we did things a little differently in Todmorden.

I believe that he ended up sending a minute sheet to the penalty office at the Halifax Road Traffic Department asking for all these fines to be made null and void in exchange for regaining some public support.

We officers were able to sleep well after sticking together as a team to defend the citizens of our town.

Unfortunately for me this little episode was to prove another turning point in my career in the force and would in due course lead to places that I could never have imagined.

Bad things were coming my way and they would change everything.

CHAPTER THREE

Death in the Afternoon

I often wonder how my life would look today if I had not been on duty on Wednesday, 11 June 1980. Most probably I would not be writing this book.

Of course, things are never that simple and we all have pivotal moments where fate arrives unforeseen and changes our destiny forever.

This was mine.

By that early summer's morning I had been a policeman for just over 5 years and received two commendations for my investigation into separate incidents that involved the deaths of three people.

One concerned a tragic road accident with multiple fatalities where the driver had fled from the scene but was eventually caught and sent to prison. The other came from another sad death which was first thought to be a suicide but eventually proved to be an accidental overdose of prescribed drugs. My police work revealing this news brought comfort to the deceased's family.

But those moments were past and on this dismal Wednesday my mood was not matching the Summer season given the atrocious weather and rain pouring down. To make matters worse I was rostered on foot patrol through the town centre. Being prepared for Pennine weather I did have my hideaways where I could escape the elements with a brew and a cigarette during a break, but walking round the town itself you would often get soaked.

So I was relieved when I got a radio message at about 4.00pm. It was muffled by my heavy raincoat – so I spoke into the mike '*10-8*' – code for asking that the message be repeated.

I then heard: '*Please attend the coal yard at Todmorden railway station .... We have a report from the ambulance station. There's a body.*'

The initial call to the ambulance crew had come from the son of the owner of the yard who had found the body on his return to work at 3.45 pm.

As I made my way on foot the Alpha Bravo 3 patrol car pulled up alongside to offer me a lift. Inside was my mate, PC Malcolm Agley, and - given the weather and the nature of the call – I gladly accepted.

We drove up to Tod railway station car park arriving there at 4.10pm and proceeded along to the far end, where we were met by Trevor Parker who had made the discovery. With him were the ambulance crew - Trevor Knight and Graham Baldwin – who had quickly responded to his call out. One of them pointed toward a very large stack of coal looming into the air beside us.

"*It's up on the top*", he said worryingly, referring to the body, "*I think there's something not quite right about it. I think you have a murder.* "

Malcolm looked at me with surprise and we made our way on foot to the coal heap. He climbed the wooden sleepers that made up the back wall of the area where the coal was retained in a pile 15 foot high, but after a few minutes came gingerly down and suggested that I should go and have a look for myself.

I will never forget the sight that confronted me - a male in his fifties and the look on his face in death was of fear and pain. The eyes were open and staring into the sky, his mouth slightly open so you could see his teeth. His hair had been cut very short into a kind of crew cut, but it was not neat, it looked like it had been done rather unprofessionally.

However, the strangest sight of all was around the rear of the skull as I inspected the man's crown - here were what looked like several small burn marks, similar in shape and size. Carefully moving the head over to one side I could see around the nape of the neck located at the base of the skull what seemed to be a large weeping wound approximately two inches in length and about one and a half inches across. There was some sort of substance smeared over the opening of this injury.

Inspecting further down the body I could see the arms were resting on top of it, not folded, but set lightly on the stomach area, just as you might place them if you were having a nap on your couch after a long day.

Another thing that immediately stood out was that the body was wearing a jacket but no shirt, just a white string vest. And, odder still, there was no sign of coal dust or dirt on the front of the body or smeared onto his face. It simply looked as if the man had lay down on his back and died – though after climbing up a sodden coal heap without somehow showing any evidence of that feat.

I concluded that the body had been dressed hurriedly after death. There was just something too odd about it and I was already ill at ease with this case. After consulting with Malcolm I discovered that he felt much the same. So we decided to call in the death as 'suspicious' and Malcolm requested that CID and a Scenes of Crime officer (SOCO) attend together with the police surgeon.

Whilst waiting for the forensic team to arrive our job now was to secure the area and preserve any evidence. We put cones around the 'Furnacite' coal heap and, as the rain was still falling hard when we finished took shelter under the coal hopper adjacent to where the body lay. Together with the ambulance crew all four of us huddled together in this makeshift refuge and discussed what we all believed to be a clear case of unexplained 'sudden death'.

It seemed an age before assistance arrived on scene, but it was just 4.25pm when first a local sergeant - Nevison - appeared along with police constable Birmingham. They brought with them Jack Parker - the owner of the yard. Police surgeon - Dr Adshead – followed at 4.36 pm and examined the body and pronounced life extinct. This formality had to be done and the time recorded even though it was obvious to us all that the person was dead.

During his examination comment was made by Dr Adshead regarding the burn marks on the dead man's head and the strange facial expression of the deceased. Indeed I believe it was the doctor who first suggested that the victim looked like he had been '*Scared to death*' – a remark that I certainly understood.

Detective Constable Pridgeon was next to arrive at 4.45pm together with local bobby - PC Campbell - and they informed that Chief Inspector Moodie - Deputy Head of the Sub-Division – was en- route with traffic patrol officer PC Ramsey – who reached the coal yard at 4.59pm.

Sergeant Ellison and PC Wilson – who were scenes of crime officers – got there at 5.11pm and started to set-up their equipment. Shortly after at 5.22pm the divisional head of CID - Detective Chief Inspector Baines - reached the location to be followed by Detective Constable Ingram at 5.37pm.

This heavy and very significant police and medical presence rapidly on scene shows that we were all taking this suspicious death very seriously indeed. In fact at 6.10 pm the official Coroners Officer - Sergeant Tetlaw – was last to appear and his presence on site was most unusual and indicative of the level of our concern.

Like I suspect did some of the others my first thought was that it probably was a murder, but not the actual scene of that murder - just the location where the body had been 'dumped' by person or persons unknown.

Inevitably, there was a lot of speculation on site, but when our searches revealed that not one item of property was on the body: - no wallet, money, or personal ID - it did look as if steps had been taken to try to slow down identification of the victim. Only after we ended these necessary searches was the body finally removed to Hebden Bridge Mortuary at 6.30pm for a Post Mortem.

Thankfully the rain started to ease around then as we made our detailed survey of the yard looking for anything that might seem to be out of place. It was very difficult as the rain had made the coal and slurry so messy and hard to walk across underfoot. But we found no footprints to suggest the man had climbed up onto the coal heap unaided.

I believe it was Malcolm Agley who discovered a tyre mark in the silt a short distance away from the base of the coal stack. This was a small indentation and, the owner told us, did not match any of the vehicles used by the coal merchant, but you could still see the tread marks and photographs of it were taken in hope that it might be a significant clue. Nor was the coal heap new . There had been no deliveries onto it that day to accidentally discard this man alongside its content.

By this point there was not a great deal else that we could do. So when nothing more turned up our search was called off at 8pm. Though I do recall the CID reminding us all that we PCs and 'not Sherlock Holmes' so it was now *their* job to take it from here and try to solve this case – which, of course, I understood.

The post mortem examination of the body was carried out at 9.15 pm by the Home Office pathologist

Dr Alan Edwards, further revealing the urgency that was being ascribed to this case. His findings were that the deceased had died of 'heart failure' due to 'ischaemic heart disease' and 'emphysema'.

Samples were taken from the body during the post mortem of what appeared to be the substance seemingly applied to the burns at the back of the man's head and neck. These samples were sealed in forensic bags and sent to the Home Office laboratory at Wetherby, North Yorkshire for detailed analysis but the substance was never identified. Dr Edwards stated that the burn appeared to result from skin contact with an 'acid, alkali or other locally destructive liquid'.

Time of death was found by Dr Edwards to be '8 – 10 hours' before his examination – therefore about 11.15 am to 1.15 pm - which was some 3 or 4 hours before discovery by Trevor Parker and my arrival on the scene. Parker confirmed being in the yard earlier that morning and that the body was not seen by him but the coal heap was easily visible and intact as he passed.

When the cause of death was reported to CID by Dr Edwards they quickly scaled things down. Because the deceased had died from apparent natural causes, as far as they were concerned it was no longer urgent and the routine enquiries were to be left to uniform division – with PC Malcolm Agley as case officer and me helping to learn if there was more to this tragedy.

One Detective Constable was involved with us as we set about first trying to identify the dead man. I will call him DC 'Dave' as he had lead authority over uniform because this remained a CID investigation, of course.

Along with PC Agley I toured local pubs and shops and even placed a photograph in the regional paper in the hope that someone would recognize the victim given that he was unfamiliar to any of the Todmorden officers from about town. But all of this investigation proved to no avail. Especially as in 1980 there was no computer network to make such cases easier to resolve.

Then - after spending many hours trawling through missing persons lists kept at many different police stations - we got lucky and finally found the identity of the deceased. He was Zygmund Jan Adamski : - a name that would go on to haunt me for a very long time.

A week after finding the body - on 18 June 1980 - DC 'Dave' and I drove over to a village called Tingley near Wakefield where the 56 year old had lived. This was well beyond our usual beat, just over 20 miles east across Yorkshire. Once there we made our way to a modest semi and hesitantly knocked on the front door.

A young man answered and invited us in. Sat in a wheelchair in the living room was an older lady who identified herself as Mrs Leokadia Adamski, but said that she preferred to be called 'Lottie'. After a brief discussion with her about the terrible discovery she agreed that a close friend of the family would come back to Hebden Bridge with us to formally identify the victim.

On that drive back over the moors we learned a lot about Zygmund from this friend, 'Chris'. He explained that Mr Adamski had gone missing on Friday the 6th June at 3.30 pm – exactly five days before the discovery of his body in Tod. As far as 'Chris' knew Mr Adamski had never been to Todmorden and had no friends or relatives living there. He was a shy person who kept himself to himself and was known to locals as 'Ziggy'. Chris could think of nobody who would do him harm.

After 'Chris' went through the sad ordeal of identifying Mr Adamski's body in the morgue he made a comment that 'Ziggy' had longer and thicker hair when he had last seen him – supporting my view that his hair had been crudely shorn recently, perhaps following the wound that he received on his head. He also pointed out that the burn like marks on the head had not been present shortly before he went missing from Tingley when Chris had last met up with his friend.

With this information added to our investigation we returned to Tingley and spoke again at more length to Mrs Adamski. She could also think of no reason why her husband would have gone missing – telling us that he was in good spirits on the day that he disappeared after going out shopping in Leeds that morning with his cousin - Laska Teodozia. Laska had been over on a holiday from Poland (where the Adamski family all originated) and had spent the last two months with them but would be returning home in a few days.

We also learned that Zygmund was due to be the best man at his god-daughter's wedding and was much looking forward to the occasion having written a speech. That wedding was the day after Zygmund went missing, making his disappearance all the more stressful for the family. Lottie and others had spent the days whilst he was missing frantically calling everyone they knew hoping to discover why he had vanished. Nobody thought of looking in Todmorden, of course, as no link has ever been traced between our town and Adamski other than it being where his body was discovered.

Things were just not adding up in this case and I was starting to ask myself a lot of questions and unsure where the answers would lead.

On the day he vanished from Tingley, Zygmund and his cousin Laska had returned from shopping in Leeds and all sat down to eat a fish and chip dinner and chatted happily over a cup of tea about the next day's wedding. Zygmund was in a jovial mood and nothing seemed to be bothering him. Then he said that he was just going to the shop 100 yards away because they needed some potatoes. Laska offered to go with him, but because the shop was so close Zygmund told her there was no need to bother. Though he had a heart condition he was generally well and doctors had told him that modest exercise was good for him. He was certainly passed fit to continue the strenuous task of being a coal mine hewer, often working the pit at nights. Something that would not have been the case if this disease had been regarded as severely compromising his health.

When Ziggy left the house to walk to the shop he did not take his car or house keys with him – just a wallet with about £20 inside. The family never saw him again and had been frantic until told the sad news that his body was found in Todmorden five days later. That wallet was never found.

Both Zygmund and Leokadia had been prisoners of war in Germany after the Nazis invaded in 1939. After liberation they moved to England like many Poles did and met in Leeds where they married in 1951 when Zygmund was 27. For 23 years he had worked down mined coal in Lofthouse colliery and was well liked by his work mates. He also loved a pint down at his local.

One of his neighbours remembered seeing him that Friday afternoon as he passed by on route to the store and recalled asking Ziggy if he was going for a drink. The miner replied cheerfully – 'No, it's too early'. His friend sensed nothing amiss and once again knew of no enemies the man might have had. But this seems to be the last conversation anyone recalls having with Adamski other than his shop purchase.

Our police investigation was getting more puzzling by the minute. So after leaving Mrs Adamski's house we visited that local shop where the shopkeeper confirmed that Zygmund had arrived and bought some groceries on that afternoon when he had gone missing. Nothing had appeared to be out of the ordinary with Zygmund during his brief visit and he seemed in a chirpy mood. The groceries he bought were never found.

None of these witnesses offered any suggestion that this man was depressed and might wander off hours before the imminent wedding. Quite the reverse as they all remarked on his good mood. So we were completely baffled about where to turn next and on the drive back to Todmorden I could not get these thoughts out of my head or come up with a logical explanation of what had happened.

Meanwhile Malcolm Agley had been busy whilst Dave and I were in Tingley. Checks were made with various health centres and hospitals to see if Zygmund was treated for his wounds or if they might have applied the unidentified 'ointment' onto him. But no records matched. At every turn this case was just one big puzzle.

Of course, in a small town rumours spread fast and every bar and café had its own 'expert' with a theory about what might have happened. There was chatter of Adamski being held captive on the moors and striking his head as he tried to flee. But no evidence was found.

That was until one day whilst I was on foot patrol in the town centre, I heard some news that made me really sit up. Peter Sutcliffe - a Station Sub Officer based at the local Fire Station in Todmorden - was also a part time worker at the Parker family coal merchants. Sutcliffe informed me that he had been present at the coal yard at between 1pm and 1.30 pm on the day that Adamski's body had been found. This was several hours after Trevor Parker had last been there with no body present. Sutcliffe had gone to the yard hoping to find Trevor, but Parker had left the site by then and Sutcliffe decided to walk down to the White Hart Fold inn and find him.

Significantly, Sutcliffe told me that Adamski's body was not on the coal heap as he walked through the yard and that surely would have seen it given that just three hours later that body was discovered in full open view.

If what Peter was telling me was true - and I had no reason to disbelieve him - then we had a key witness with regards to the arrival of the body. This was discovered by Trevor at 3.45pm who until then had been away from the yard since 8.30am that day. Parker confirmed meeting Sutcliffe at the White Hart Fold at around 1.30pm but they had not returned to the yard until Parker went back alone some two hours later.

So if Adamski was not there between 1 and 1.30 pm

as Peter Sutcliffe's story indicates and the post mortem says Adamski died between 11.15 am and 1.15 pm this evidence strongly supports the view that the man was dead *before* arriving on the coal heap.

If so then somebody took him there and placed his body in the yard before Parker returned.

It was also relevant that the coal was in view of trains passing through and stopping at the adjacent rail station making it improbable that a body could lay there all day whilst Parker was away without someone on the platform having seen it. So this was crucial evidence.

I took all of this information back to the Police station and informed CID at Halifax expecting them now to investigate further but instead was rebuffed:-

'He died of natural causes, just let it be'.

Some days later I talked to PC Agley about this evidence and he was of the same mind that the new witness information should be followed up by CID. But after speaking with 'Dave' - our DC lead - the same lack of interest was reported again.

'Sorry, Alan, but now that we have identified the body and because Adamski died from natural causes, there really is not much else we can do'.

Having spent much time with Lottie Adamski and her family during those tragic days I found it hard to let this rest. I felt she deserved my personal effort to try to find answers to her many questions. So I put pen to paper and submitted what is known in the police as a 'minute sheet' :- a form of official report. Such minute sheets are submitted through the Chief Superintendent, head of the divisional headquarters at Halifax. I thought that this would hopefully make sure the new evidence was at least placed on record for whatever official enquiries that got underway.

Some days later I was called into the station where a very senior CID officer whom I had never seen before but was apparently over from Halifax told me in no uncertain terms I must '*leave well alone'*. Fearing that I had unwittingly trodden on someone's toes, of course I did so as this was a CID matter but felt sad that Mrs Adamski and her family might not get closure.

Soon afterwards on foot patrol at night I had cause to visit the Fire Station and found that Peter Sutcliffe was by chance on duty. Over a pot of tea we discussed the 'Adamski' case and he informed me that he had visited the police station to make an official statement just as I suggested that he should. A 'CID man from Halifax' was sent to take his report and was then informed that following this statement he could be called as a witness by any subsequent inquest. Given the importance of his account over how and when Adamski's body got onto the coal tip we both expected that would happen. Yet it never did.

Bemused by all of this I just got on with my job. Until one evening in late September I was sitting down to have a meal break in the mess room when PC Malcolm Agley came in and asked me if I had seen the local paper. I had not but he showed me an article on the front page stating that coroner - James Turnbull - had held and concluded the inquest and recorded an 'Open Verdict' on the death of Zygmund Adamski.

We both looked shocked. Malcolm had attended a first brief session in July before it was quickly adjourned for a full CID investigation to report back. But he had not been recalled as a witness or even told that it had been reconvened for such detailed hearings – and I had never been called to give any evidence at all – and neither had key witness Sutcliffe.

PC Agley contacted the coroner's office in Halifax and was told that he had 'not been needed' so was never informed. He was surprised given that he was official case officer reporting to the coroner.

Over the years both Malcolm and I have wondered if we could have done more to unravel this tragedy. But we feel that we did all we could as our ability to involve ourselves was limited by this being a CID led case. Though, as Peter Sutcliffe was never called to give evidence despite his importance to the time line it is surprising that seemingly crucial testimony was never put on record before the coroner.

The first session of the inquest was held at the Calderdale court in Halifax less than a month after the tragedy – 3 July 1980. Mrs Adamski was present at this and the subsequent sessions and frequently expressed frustration with not knowing what had happened to her husband.

The initial hearing was simply given over to Dr Alan Edwards, the pathologist from Halifax Infirmary, providing testimony under oath about his findings. He reported a number of important points.

Firstly, that Adamski was clean and well cared for

and did not appear to have been sleeping rough during the missing five days. He only had one days beard growth, seemingly had been eating during his disappearance but had not eaten on the day he died. He had slight abrasions on the body but nothing suggesting that he had ever been seriously assaulted. Dr Edwards confirmed that death was in his view caused by heart failure and underlying heart disease but agreed that this could well have been triggered by something like excessive exertion or fear or even stress of fending off an attack.

The burn mark caused by a 'hot or corrosive liquid' or an acid was, the doctor stated, likely two days old - so probably happened mid-way through Adamski's five day disappearance. Lottie Adamski stated in court that she thought her husband looked to have been scared to death and that he was a 'good man' and in her view 'somebody took him and dumped him'. But this was never seemingly considered in detail in court.

Chris, the family friend who had accompanied me back to Hebden Bridge to identify the body, also gave evidence under oath. He explained how Ziggy had been trying to get permission for early retirement from the pit (which ironically would soon close down anyway thanks to Margaret Thatcher's mining purge). He had asked for this early exit because of his wife's deteriorating disability and a desire to serve as her full time carer. But the coal board had not yet reached a final decision – and with a sad twist of fate actually gave that approval in a letter that arrived during the five days he was missing.

In answering questions from the coroner Chris confirmed no family connection with Todmorden and that he was sure to have known if Ziggy was involved in anything untoward. He added that Adamski was utterly devoted to his wife. Something that was obvious to me from my time with her.

On oath Lottie confirmed that her husband had left the house wearing a striped jacket and a sports shirt and had a watch, driving licence and money – all things that were never found. He had not gone missing in the 30 years she had known him. The pathologist also confirmed in answer to questions posed that there was no evidence of brain injury or stroke to suggest that Mr Adamski could have 'lost his memory' or gone wandering over those days when his location remains a mystery.

After brief comments as to how police initiated the investigation the obviously puzzled coroner stated that he found the case 'intractable' and that they should not '*leave any stone unturned*' whilst investigating the matter further. He added that '*whatever can be done will be done – I shall see that it is done*.'

With this he adjourned proceedings leaving PC Agley sure that he would be called back when the inquest was ready to resume and further evidence had been gathered such as from key witness Peter Sutcliffe. But, as we saw, Malcolm was not recalled and Sutcliffe was never called at all – and nor was I. We all got to read about the verdict in the paper!

On 4 September 1980 the second session was held. It largely comprised Detective Inspector Boyle of Sowerby Bridge reporting on the CID investigation. This had evidently found very little.

Local hospitals do not seem to have treated Mr Adamski during his missing five days. Several eminent doctors had been consulted on the 'burn' marks and concurred it was likely caused by a corrosive liquid but could not say what it was or if it was self-administered or deliberate or accidental.

DI Boyle disagreed with Mrs Adamski that her husband's body had been dumped in Todmorden by someone else, and insisted that he believed the man '*died where he was found'*. But he had no idea how he got there. The contradiction to this conclusion of Sutcliffe being present after medical time of death and seeing no body then present was never even brought to the coroner's attention.

The final session came on 25 September 1980 and was entirely given over to several friends and relatives of Mrs Adamski discussing local tittle tattle over a theory of what might have occurred. This testimony appeared to eliminate such lines of enquiry to the satisfaction of the coroner.

In conclusion he admitted complete frustration – saying that '*at this stage there is just nothing else I can do*.' But that the case was by '*no means closed'*.

However, as far as the legal pursuit of the truth that appears to be unfortunately what it did mean because nothing further has ever appeared in evidence to my knowledge.

The inquest found an Open Verdict and the case officially remains unresolved over 37 years later.

My own opinion as to why Adamski was found dead on the top of that coal heap on a wet Wednesday afternoon in Todmorden is simple. He was placed there by someone. He certainly did not arrive there under his own steam. And if time of death is accurate he did not die where he was found either. But it seems as if we might never know the tragic circumstances under which he met his fate.

I spoke many times to Malcolm Agley regarding this case and also with other officers that were involved and without exception we feel sad that Mrs Adamski never learned that truth. My suspicion over the years is that speculation linking the death with aliens did not help any further investigation – a daft theory with no obvious substance whatsoever.

But who first raised this odd possibility - and why?

Jenny Randles is a researcher into strange phenomena whom I have known since 1981. She was born near Bacup just across the moors from Tod and has investigated many local cases. In 1983 she published a book about strange lights seen in this area and has worked hard to help me to get this book into print over the past year, adding in some of her own local case investigations.

Jenny first mentioned the Adamski case in print and admits was accidentally to blame for the media getting wind of this. But that was a year *after* the inquest ended, so she could not have influenced the coroner or police investigations into it as they had all ended by then.

Having first discovered the Adamski case via the local newspaper coverage following the inquest Jenny was drawn to the fact that the widowed Lottie was left wheelchair bound seeking answers. Her father was wheelchair bound from her childhood and later her mother was too after a stroke so Lottie's plight was one she understood.

It was also the sort of mystery explored by the popular ITV programme - Strange But True? - for which Jenny later worked as story consultant. Indeed, through her, I became the main subject of the pilot episode of this show that at its height attracted 12 million viewers.

For someone interested in UFOs the Todmorden death was made more intriguing by Ziggy's name. Adamski is unusual in England, though more common in Poland. Yet George Adamski was one of the most famous UFO witnesses on the planet. During the 1950s he claimed to have been taken away by aliens and had meetings in the Californian desert with beings from another world. He wrote several books on his experience and later claimed to have been invited by famous people such as the Pope to have a private audience and pass on messages he was allegedly given by the tall humanoid beings he encountered.

This man's stories are widely regarded - even in UFO circles - as far more colourful than they are credible but they did influence the early years of public interest in 'flying saucers'.

There was also another connection. Several famous UFO abductions - where a person disappears and returns to tell of an alien kidnap - feature a period of 5 days during which they are missing just as here.

One of the best known examples is of logger Travis Walton, who disappeared on 5 November 1975 from Snowflake, Arizona, after his work crew witnessed a UFO. This led to his colleagues being suspected by police of his murder until he reappeared on 10 November. His story was subsequently retold as a Hollywood movie 'Fire in the Sky'.

Jenny had also already investigated a number of UFO reports in and around Todmorden and one was near the centre around midnight on 10 June 1980. This was just half a mile from where Adamski's body turned up on that coal heap hours later. A young couple had reported hearing a strange noise over their house – '*like great water surges moving to and fro'*. Going outside they could see nothing causing the sound as it faded slowly into the distance – until an ellipse of light appeared above their roof and glowed both green and red before seemingly climbing vertically and disappearing.

The couple had wanted no publicity and the team of Manchester UFO investigators that Jenny worked with suspected that this might just have been a helicopter above low cloud and mist preceding the heavy rain when I was at the coal yard with Adamski's body next day.

Helicopters working on the power lines with searchlights had caused a few UFO sightings. So this Tod case was at the time not pursued much beyond recording the details.

Of course when the press reported the news that Adamski body was discovered nearby the sighting looked more interesting. There was absolutely nothing to directly link these two events beyond coincidence and past UFO lore and some rather imaginative speculation.

Jenny has always emphasised this. But once the Manchester team started to research my experiences they discovered that with PC Agley I had been the first on scene at the Adamski case investigation. That made things even more intriguing though, again, only further coincidences not facts.

In her short summary for the UFO community Jenny placed both events together for the first time. Her one page review was only published in a specialist UFO magazine called Flying Saucer Review under the title:- 'A policeman's lot'. That was in August 1981 after the police file and inquest had been over by nearly 12 months. Her account focused almost entirely on events you will read in following chapters that the Manchester group were now investigating and only mentioned Adamski in passing as being '*a preliminary teaser*'.

The research group had met with Lottie Adamski and tried to help her find some answers that she was still desperately seeking after the failure of the inquest, but they soon decided that they sadly must drop this pursuit because, tragic as it was, it had – as Jenny stated in her report - '*no apparent relevance*' to the main UFO mystery that they were now investigating.

Jenny also points out that – despite my name and a photograph in police uniform having appeared in the local press – she did not identify me in her report as the Manchester group adhered to a code of practice that protected witness identity. They were still working with me on my story and knew that as a police officer I was under some pressure not to talk in public, so Jenny decided to keep it low key and leave further investigation into Adamski to the police.

'In retrospect', Jenny tells me, *'I probably should not have connected these two events – even though it was just for a UFO journal whose readers would know why I did. I was not linking them anywhere in public and kept your identity anonymous and never suggested that Adamski was abducted by aliens because it was not our conclusion at the Manchester UFO Research Association that he was. We only tried to help Lottie after the inquest ended without giving her resolution.'*

About a month after that Flying Saucer Review report appeared members of the Manchester group started to receive calls from a reporter at a tabloid. Jenny was on holiday with her fiancé at a caravan site in the remote North Wales countryside and in 1981 there were no mobile phones, of course. Yet that paper kept calling the camp offices after tracking Jenny down so that she could identify 'the policeman'.

Despite being offered inducements to talk Jenny declined to assist the newspaper. Other Manchester group investigators also refused requests that they should divulge my identity. It seems that Jenny's article had been read by a Yorkshire UFO enthusiast who got excited by the possible causes of the Adamki death. The reporter followed this up on their suggestion and facts got garbled in an attempt to uncover more because Jenny was refusing to break her promise of confidentiality and so they could not speak with me. The West Yorkshire police also declined to name me, when asked by the paper, who told them that *their* 'investigators' had 'uncovered' my story.

The result was a front page article talking about a

'*UFO Death Riddle'* - claiming that UFO researchers termed the Adamski case a Close Encounter of the Third Kind (which would mean that he had met an alien!)

There was also some rather misleading information seemingly guessed about me but could have put people on the wrong track if they were looking for my identity.

Jenny felt rather guilty after this episode and learned lessons about the media because of its consequences as did we all.

In fact the Manchester group even stopped talking with the tabloids about ongoing cases in order to avoid such a problem. They focused cooperation on working with media sources only as part of efforts to raise money for charity. As in this photo taken a little later where you see Jenny Randles and some other members of the Manchester team then working at Jodrell Bank Radio Telescope in Cheshire for a weekend. Here Jenny gave lectures on UFOs to the public in the planetarium and the group sold UFO research material to raise a large sum as part of an ITV telethon. The temptation to raise funds for investigation by helping the tabloids with stories ended and was replaced by this.

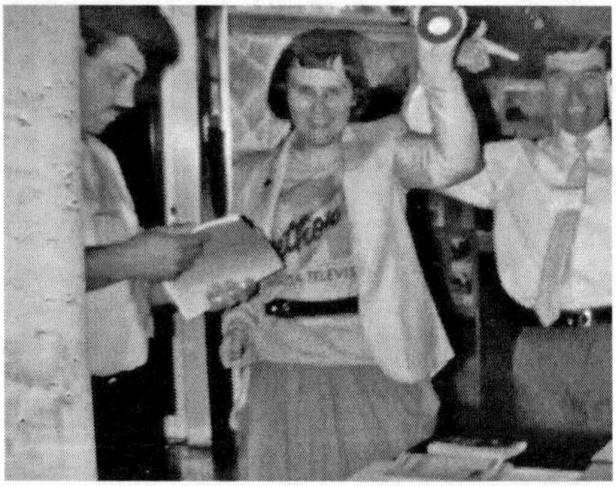

Regardless of such subsequent benefits the appearance of that front page headline in 1981 had ensured that the Adamski death then became linked with UFOs across the world. And it did so in a rather garbled manner because of a UFO investigator whose identity we still do not know because the paper declined to reveal their source despite expecting Jenny to identify me to them as a serving police officer.

Once this alien link found its way into public thinking alongside the Adamski case there was no real way of taking it back. It had become part of the case.

UFOs are easily dismissed as nonsense and can take a genuine mystery with them just by being mentioned in the same context. Especially when the UFO elements of the Adamski case were overplayed by the press.

In fact whilst the inquest was long over by this point – the coroner James Turnbull was even persuaded to give a quote to the paper saying that he depended on facts during his assessment of all such cases like this one, but unfortunately had not been able to uncover any of them to resolve the Adamski affair. And although he had always expected a simple answer to be found none ever was.

He even noted a personal observation to the paper on the bizarre theory about Adamski's death being linked by 'UFO' buffs with aliens :

'I must admit that if I was walking over Ilkley Moor and a UFO came down I would not be surprised. I might be terrified but not surprised.'

Of course a year earlier in 1980 when we at the Todmorden police department were investigating the Adamski tragedy any talk of aliens as the cause of this poor man's death – however speculative - would have been viewed by us all as nonsense.

At the time of the police investigation and coroner's inquest it was easy for us to laugh off any thought of alien abduction let alone it being part of this tragedy. It was just not common sense thinking in the tradition of the police force where you considered the rational possibilities to solve a case rather than the absurdities.

But such understandably sober views about aliens and UFOs were about to come back to bite in a way that the West Yorkshire police could never have imagined.

And I would be right in the thick of it forcing me to reassess all my jocular thoughts about extraordinary phenomena.

CHAPTER FOUR

A Close Encounter

After the traumatic months of the Adamski enquiry I tried to get back into my usual routine when winter 1980 arrived. Frankly I just kept my head down at work. The last thing I wanted was more confrontation with my bosses. Nor was I expecting anything other than a series of mundane events whilst out on patrol.

Such hopes were quickly dashed by fate as something happened in our quiet little town that would become news around the world. It would change my life in a way that I could never have imagined.

Looking back after all these years I still have difficulty taking in what occurred completely out of the blue in just a few short moments. At times I find myself asking if it really did happen. But I know, of course, that it did!

November meant that the leaves had fallen from the trees and the Pennine weather was at its wet and miserable worst. We seemed to be heading for another damp, freezing winter. The nights were really drawing in and the milder days of summer seemed a lifetime away.

I had been on night duty for nearly a week and seen no daylight to speak of for what seemed like an age. Such a late shift during long winters was often depressing and had an insidious effect on your metabolism. We humans need to recharge our batteries and if you are working overnight then you sleep your way through shorter days and never seem to get an adrenaline boost. Studies in northern latitudes like the far reaches of Alaska where nights can go on for weeks before the Sun rises again have found this can even make you physically ill. So nightshift during that chilly November was to be endured rather than enjoyed.

On the night of Friday 28 November 1980 I had not been on duty long when around midnight the station received a call from a resident at a local council estate reporting that a herd of cows were wandering around the houses causing a nuisance. Nothing much else was happening so it was a job that we would follow up even though that might not be possible with busier forces.

As I drove up to the estate I received a report that another resident had phoned the station to make a similar claim about these cattle. So I drove about and went up and down every avenue but there was no sign of any marauding cows. I reported back to the station that these calls might well be a hoax.

It was a very wet night outside and the rain was pouring down heavily at times. My windscreen wipers on the patrol car were working furiously and you had to keep the de-misters running constantly to get a clear view ahead.

Having put the matter aside by around 1 am on Saturday 29 November I received a further radio message to go back to the estate because a third resident had now reported being awakened by loud noises coming from her garden.

This lady was one of the more elderly occupants of those streets, who offered me a cup of tea upon my arrival and - being known never to refuse an offer like that - I cheerily agreed. So over a nice cuppa she described to me what had occurred and I made a promise not to laugh at what she wanted to say.

"*I know I'm old but I'm not bloody senile*" she started to explain - which made me smile. What she told me in confidence I have kept secret up to now in order to prevent her from becoming a figure of fun.

Slowly she revealed that she had been awakened by strange noises outside in her garden. Peering through the bedroom window she had seen five or six cows moving about in the dark and so decided to call the police.

When she went downstairs to use the phone located on the front window ledge she pulled open the curtains slightly to describe what the beasts were doing. But just as she was putting the receiver down after calling there was a very strange event. She described it as an extremely bright glow – like a car headlight that had suddenly gone onto full beam. It lit up the window and just a second later all went dark again. Looking back out at her garden the cows had vanished

I told this rather flummoxed lady that a car somewhere nearby had probably just passed over a rise and its light had frightened the cows away. She nodded at what seemed like a logical suggestion. However, little did either of us know at that moment that her account was going to prove far more significant when the events of that night continued.

Of course, with three reports now confirming that these pesky cattle were out there it was clearly not a hoax. So I made another full search of the estate but once again found there were not any cows in sight and returned to the station full of frustration. I decided this could only be described as a 'no trace' incident – which was where no follow up action was deemed necessary without immediate need for an official report.

As that long nightshift dragged on towards the distant dawn it finally stopped raining, but a very low cloud cover had come in after the downpour, sweeping over the valley bottom and making it all feel rather eerie. Thankfully nobody else had reported further sightings of those mysterious cows.

I had just finished some paperwork in the office with one of my colleges and was about to drive down toward the town centre to check things out in the deserted streets when he informed me that he was going to sign off duty an hour early now it was 5 am.

We left the station together and he headed off to the police flats nearby. Then I drove down into the town centre and watched the staff bus heading from Burnley Road having picked up early morning crew and heading to the Yorkshire Metro garage ready to take out the first service buses heading for places like Halifax. It was a common sight for me on these early turns. As he passed me by I think I gave the driver a wave as I often did when I knew him locally. On those early morning shifts when it was deathly quiet about town any familiarity was always welcome.

The driver nodded back to me and in Tod centre I then met another officer who was on foot patrol in the still soggy streets. I pulled up alongside him and he informed me that he had just checked all the shops and buildings for signs of trouble and that everything was in order.

So, not being needed here, I told him that I was going to drive up to the council estate and have one last look 'for those bloody cows'. He laughed on hearing my tale about the 'major' incident that had plagued the neighbourhood throughout the night . So I set off toward Burnley Road and remember asking if he wanted to get out of the chilly air and join me in the warm just for the ride. But he shook his head.

How much have I wished since then that he had answered differently, because it would have been priceless for me to have had another officer by my side and share in what was about to happen on that journey.

Instead I drove off on my own unsuspecting of what lay ahead or that I would have to face all the flak heading my way without back up.

It was now about ten past five in the morning as I drove up Burnley Road heading north-west a few hundred yards out of town and passing the police station on my right hand side before I did.

After half a mile or so I neared Ferney Lee Road

which would take me on a right turn off the main highway up toward the estate where the cattle had been apparently running amok. Those houses looked down from an elevated position onto the narrow valley cut by Burnley Road alongside the River Calder.

As I approached the junction I had my right traffic indicator on preparing for this turn when something caught my eye further on – several hundred yards or so ahead. I was momentarily unsure what it might be and immediately thought of the local staff bus and that it might have been in an accident to get slewed sideways across the road. But then I remembered that I had already seen it pass in town and it was still too early for any of the actual service buses to be running.

Even as I was puzzling this out during what was probably just a few seconds all thought of this simple explanation disappeared because on closing in I could see very clearly that the thing was a completely different shape to any bus.

Instinctively I abandoned the plan to drive up Ferney Lee road and instead carried on up Burnley Road heading straight towards this 'thing' that I could now see was completely blocking the main road ahead.

As I inched closer I slowed right down to just a crawl and was gawping at the object right there in front of me because I could not believe what I was seeing. Then I rolled to a full stop close enough for it to now almost fill my windscreen and yet still be completely incomprehensible.

'*What the hell is this?*' I was saying to myself.

The large object was just hanging there in the air only about five feet off the road surface and I was no more than twenty yards away so easily able to take in full details of its appearance. I could see it was definitely *not* a bus!

Instead I realized that it looked like something out of the ' recent Star Wars' movie - a diamond shaped object about twenty feet wide and fourteen feet in height with what appeared to be a row of dark paneling across the upper top third of it - although what I took to be paneling might also have been darkened windows. My headlights were shining off and illuminating the side.

What I do know is that I could have gotten out of my patrol car and thrown a brick at the thing to find out if it went clang! That missed opportunity has always annoyed me - but there was no way I was brave enough to have attempted such a feat in this extraordinary situation far beyond any routine police patrol.

As I was staring at the object before me there seemed a florescent glow coming from a large dome on top and the whole thing was spinning slowly in an anti-clockwise direction. It's overall colour resembled unpolished gunmetal.

For a few moments I just sat there staring in awe not knowing what on Earth I was going to do about this impossible situation. I was trained to dealing with the unexpected and used to being in control of my reactions from any circumstance that was sprung upon me, but this was just outside any of the police rule books.

Then as I watched it still spinning I noticed that the

dark brown leaves that had fallen from nearby trees beside the highway were spiraling upwards around the object in an eerie dance that took them in a clockwise direction. The branches of the trees between the road and the river were also blowing about as though there was a very strong wind causing them to do this and yet – when I had got into the patrol car a few minutes earlier and half a mile away there was no noticeable wind at all.

This whole thing was so weird.

Some semblance of my duty as a police officer pushed its way into my consciousness at this point. This object was blocking the road. So, quite probably was my car parked there in front of it as I just stared at it. There could be other traffic coming towards us even though the area was often deserted at this hour.

So my training kicked in and to be safe I put on my blue flashing beacon atop the patrol car and flipped on hazard warning lights. Then I attempted to radio the local control room at Sowerby Bridge police station and somehow explain what I was watching. But nothing happened. For some reason I was unable to establish contact using my UHF personal radio set.

Okay, I thought, I know that is not too unusual as the deep valley bottom where Todmorden is situated can make signals hard to get through. So I decided to try again using the police vehicle's VHF radio – which I knew to be more able to communicate through difficult 'dead zones' like this. That signal went to the force's area's control centre at Bradford.

But once again I was unable to make any contact

even via this system. When I tried later in this same spot there was no problem making contact with either type of radio reception. So for both communication methods to fail together during the proximity of this object hovering in front of me - that certainly was unexpected.

Unsure what to do next, I considered getting the hell out of there back to town. I really wanted to bring someone else out here to see what I was watching and tell me that I was not going mad. But experience took over and calmed me down so I decided the next best thing was to make a sketch of what was in front of me with approximate measurements for the official record. This was much like I would do if coming on the scene of an RTA (road traffic accident). So I picked up my clipboard, which officers took with them when operating one of the patrol cars in order to log vehicular incidents.

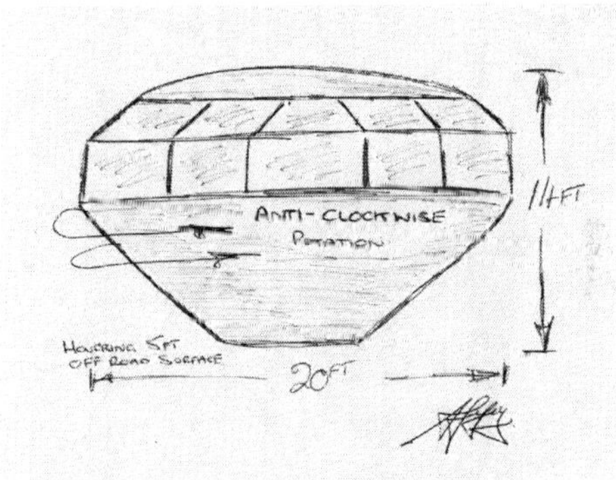

Here is what I drew.

Of course, that pad was used to sketch road vehicles involved in an incident - not bloody great flying things that are rotating above the main road. But there was some foolscap paper on the clipboard. So I used this to draw on, but only remember starting my sketch depicting what was still sitting there right in front of me.

Then suddenly as I finished the outline something else remarkable happened. There was a brilliant white flash of light out of nowhere that scared the hell out of me. It was so blinding that everything went black – a bit like having a photograph taken with a flashgun thrust in front of your face whilst you are in a dark cellar – only here it was multiplied by a thousand times.

I only joined the dots and realized when back home later how this dramatic event was just like what the old lady had described happening to her on the estate above the valley road here just a few hours earlier when the cows had suddenly disappeared from her garden.

With that burst of light my view of reality suddenly turned on its head. No longer was I sat there looking at the object directly ahead and sketching it for posterity. I now found myself driving the patrol car up Burnley Road maybe a hundred yards beyond the other side of where the thing had been hovering.

I had no idea how this 'switch' just happened or if I even drove 'through' the object - but a glance in the rear view mirror told me that it was no longer over the road.

Shaking my head trying to comprehend what was going on I turned the car round and drove back to where the thing had been floating and for the first time parked up and gingerly stepped into the night. I looked nervously around not quite sure what might leap out from roadside bushes. My eyes were everywhere looking for a sign of movement or any cue to jump back into the car and get the hell out of there. But – I admit – I was mainly gazing upwards at this point - into the dark night sky - wondering if whatever it was went that-a-way.

There was still a very low cloud cover and that strange tingly electric feeling about the place that was tickling my senses almost as if it was touching my skin. Glancing down to the road surface below me I could also clearly see that this was bone dry – but only right below where that object had hovered. Everywhere else the tarmac was still glistening wet from the earlier rain.

Another thing that stood out was a whirlpool like shape around this same dry spot – where leaves and other twigs and small branches had been scattered around in this pattern as they had swirled about the object. It was very peculiar.

By now the fact that I was in this spot all on my own suddenly hit me. I felt vulnerable, so jumped back into the car and drove off with a screech of tyres – racing towards the station to seek help. As I pulled up outside the police station PC Malcom Agley was just about to go in after ending his own patrol, so I blew the horn at him and with the window now wound down shouted for him to get in the passenger seat.

He looked puzzled and pointed to his wristwatch to suggest he was going off duty but came toward the car where I just repeated - '*Jump in*!'

I did a fast u-turn on the road and shot off at speed back toward the exact spot now deeply etched in my memory. Malcolm moaned about his shift being over, but I did not take much notice of what he was saying as I was in such a hurry to get back there and show him what had just happened.

My colleague probably thought that I was mad as I

babbled about what had occurred on that short drive back down Burnley Road - but when we got to the site we both got out and looked around. Even he could see how the road surface was bone dry and there was a strange swirl of leaves and everything.

I explained in detail what I had seen as we both bent down rather carefully to feel the road surface where these marks were positioned. I assumed it was maybe 10 minutes since I had seen the thing hovering but the markings were still noticeably warm to the touch – weird in the chill late November air.

We both then stood at this spot where in this 1982 photo you can see me pointing to the place where the UFO had hovered.

Whilst looking at all of this one of us suggested going into Centre Vale park situated next to the road beyond the river. This was over a stone wall beside the spot where Jenny Randles is standing when taking the photograph of me above. We just wanted to see if anyone was there who might have witnessed the event.

However, in those days the gates were locked at

night and there was also the problem of the deep river bed which ran the full length of the park and separated it completely from Burnley Road. Access was not going to be easy.

Undeterred we climbed over the tall gates and scrambled into the fields, moving slowly along the path guided only by our flashlights. We turned and faced the Rugby pitch situated about fifty yards away - beams from our torches darting to and fro to light the darkness.

Nobody was in the park at that hour, of course. But something else was with us.

We both jumped back in shock as my torch illuminated the lumbering outline of a cow – or actually it was half a dozen cows.

No cattle were ever grazed in the park. Were these the same herd that I had been looking for all night? And if so how the hell did they get over here across a main road, the River Calder and the locked gates?

I could not think of any logical explanation.

There was no sign at all of the object that had been hovering just yards away above the main road minutes earlier so after a brief discussion we decided that it was best to return to the station. But by the time we signed off it was around 6.30 am and we were half an hour late finishing our tour of duty and the morning staff had already arrived and taken over.

I did briefly notice that this seemed rather odd but I was not sure how long we had wandered in the park trying to find marks in the wet earth to suggest how the cattle had got into there. So I did not immediately realise that there was anything very wrong about the time.

Needless to say the morning shift at the police station started quizzing us both on where we had been when we should have long since 'clocked off'. There were raised eyebrows and some humorous banter when I told them the full story, but I could not blame them for finding it odd. In their shoes I would probably have acted exactly the same.

So, accepting it all in good form, I set off home.

I was completely bemused by these events and was trying to get my head around facing such a strange thing completely without warning. Just glad to sit down I reflected over a nice cup of strong tea in the safety of my own house where I could take my heavy police boots off and try to relax.

But as I took off my boots I noticed for the first time an irritating itch to the instep of my left foot. After removing my sock I could now see that there was a small round reddish mark at this spot that was about an inch across. I gave it a good scratch but it still itched so I dabbed some antiseptic cream onto the wound in an attempt to help, but it made no difference. Then I noticed there was a split in the sole of my left boot which was lying on its side on the floor.

On closer examination I found that the split had gone right through to the inner sole and covered the full width of the boot. To this day I have no idea how such a thing could have happened. These were relatively new Doc Marten boots that I was only just breaking in. They were not like this when I went on my shift, but it looked as if I had been dragged on the floor sometime after.

In Jenny Randles' photo you can see the damage.

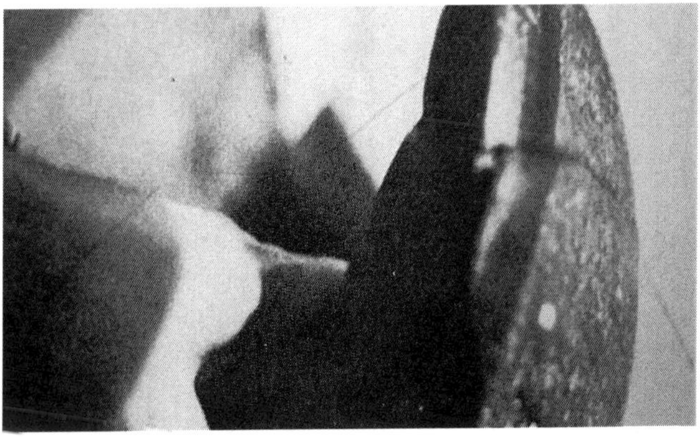

I tossed the boots aside and went to bed, sleeping soundly but briefly and was up and before noon. Then I discovered that one of my colleges had revealed my story to others when meeting them around town.

'*So it wasn't a dream?*' I muttered - mostly to myself when told.

My first thought on waking up was that the previous night's events which flooded into my head had not really happened and I was just remembering a vivid nightmare still lingering as dreams do. Now I knew differently.

It was a strange feeling, a bit like if you have swallowed lots of ale the night before and the lads describe how you did something daft 'under the influence' but you can't remember much about it. Then the flashbacks start and you know – however silly – that those antics were not just imagination.

'*So it really happened?*" , I kept saying to myself, hoping it might make this absurdity just go away.

After a while I went to pick-up my two kids, which I often did after night duty. It was always nice to see them as sometimes you never got to spend much time with them given the shift patterns in the Police. I was in two minds whether or not to mention the 'Flying Saucer' but decided they were too young to understand.

Getting ready for my next shift of duty that evening I began to feel more nervous about the prospect. To be blunt I was anxious over meeting my colleagues and what their reactions would be. Especially given the recent fuss over the Adamski death my concerns were also quite real about what my bosses might have to say given this latest leap far outside the routine world of police business.

Would they all think I was finally going bonkers? Well I was about to find out.

"*Hey up, it's captain Kirk*" one of my fellow bobbies said as I entered the station whilst others started to giggle.

I barked back a quick oath and went straight to the parade room to look at my inbox to see if there was anything new in there.

A colleague, PC John Allen, had followed me in:

'*Take no notice of them prats*" he said.

I nodded at him with a shrug, knowing he was meaning well.

"*The Inspector wants to see you, he's up in his office,*" John added.

As I knocked on the officer's door I thought 'What the hell is he going to say - probably ask me if I had been drinking.' Which I never did on duty, of course.

"*Come In*" the inspector said loudly, followed by, more softly, "*Sit down and tell me what happened last night, Alan.*"

'Alan?' I thought - that is unusual as it would normally be PC Godfrey.

Anyway I sat down to relate the events of the previous night, fully expecting him to start laughing at any point or at least come out with some sarcastic remark.

But – no - he just sat there taking notes.

"*Are you sure about the times*" he said in a very serious voice as if getting it straight for the record.

I explained that I was and also then asked why?

He then went on to tell me about an incident that had occurred on the moors above Halifax involving three other officers from their local police station. This had been advised to him officially when my account had been called through to HQ by the morning shift.

This happened – as we both then believed based on

what Halifax had told the inspector – at 4.49 am and so about 20 minutes earlier on the same morning as my own encounter. In fact, years later, on release of the file from the records at the Ministry of Defence in Whitehall about this case, it turned out to have actually been a few days earlier. But in any case I was so relieved not to be alone in seeing something over Burnley Road.

Clearly the police knew something was flying around and did not now just have my word for that. So my own account was being officially recorded to add to the one from Halifax.

PC John Porter - a dog handler - and PC Howard Turnpenny - together with WPC Julie Baxter - had all driven up onto the moors above Halifax to search for some stolen motorbikes that they believed to have been hidden by persons in their custody on suspicion of their theft. They were scouring some kennels at Cold Edge Dam between Halifax and Hebden Bridge.

Whist making their way up onto the moor tops PC Porter became aware of a 'steel blue' pulsating light which appeared to be following them as they drove. It was hovering just below the cloud cover and moving across the skyline.

When they reached their destination all three officers got out of their respective patrol cars and PC Turnpenny asked PC Porter if he had noticed the light as they arrived. They then all stood there watching it as it made a large sweeping arc across the sky beneath the low thick cloud.

Suddenly it appeared to turn and swoop down

towards them before moving off at great speed across the hillside in the general direction of Todmorden.

WPC Baxter said later that it was a very strange object and – given how oddly it moved across the sky she did not think it was any kind of aircraft. This was also the opinion of both PC Turnpenny and PC Porter.

They all reported the incident on their return to the station at Halifax. In fact PC Porter insisted that a report be put onto the Chief Constable's daily log sheet. This was a 24hr information blotter which recorded the most important incidents that had occurred during that day and which were deemed necessary to bring to the Chief Constable's attention.

No wonder my inspector was taking me seriously given how Tod station had been quickly informed of this unexpected back up by Force Control in Bradford.

I was delighted to have this corroboration from other police officers. It made such a difference as I was not alone in 'seeing things'. The Inspector now told me to make a full report on what I had observed and together with my sketch made on the accident clip board - submit it '*Under cover*'.

That meant it would be addressed to the Chief Superintendent at Halifax.

After I did as requested I carried on with my duties now sporting a huge smile across my face. 'No more piss-taking from that lot' I thought to myself. But questions were still buzzing around my own head.

What had happened? What on Earth was it that I

had seen? Where did it come from and where the hell did it go to when it suddenly disappeared?

More dramatically I was now waking up to realise the extraordinary manner with which I 'jumped' from one spot on Burnley Road to another in what seemed like an instant when that beam of light had been 'fired' straight into my eyes.

Then there were the cows. How did they get into the park across a road and river and locked gates? The only remotely credible route would have had them negotiate a very steep set of steps and numerous other obstacles. It was just about possible to conceive that one cow might make that trek but they would all have had to be equally nimble in the dark. It seemed absurd and it was quite a long way for them to have travelled after leaving the estate without being spotted again given how often they had awoken the locals earlier.

There were so many unanswered questions here.

Another was the itch on my left instep. It was not getting any better and became a deeper reddish colour as the night wore on. I was out in the patrol car on that evening with PC John Allen and naturally we talked constantly about the events from 24 hours earlier as he was eager to know my story first hand, but I was a bit surprised by his laid back attitude on the subject.

John explained this by telling me about an incident that he had witnessed personally whilst serving in the Royal Navy on manoeuvers in the Atlantic.

A group of bright lights had appeared in the sky and

seemed to be following their ship for a distance. They were also picked up on the vessel's radar. The crew had then been put on alert to keep eyes on those lights and watch what they did - until they just blinked out and disappeared. He thought they had witnessed a group of UFO's that were observing this naval exercise, but had no idea what version the captain would include in any official report.

Of course, neither did I know what my police file was going to say!

Going back to the scene of the previous night's encounter was quite strange. It felt as though nothing had really happened on this spot, everything just seemed so normal now. No marks were visible on the highway. I could hardly believe that right where I was now standing a large diamond shaped UFO had been hovering no more than five foot off the ground.

I drove back up to the estate above the valley to the spot where the cows had been last reported. Here you could see just how far it was from where they eventually turned up. I drove the car around to look for a path where the cows might have taken without being seen. But there was no logical way that might allow them to cover that distance.

Whilst having my evening meal break back at the station and going over all these questions in my head something suddenly occurred to me. So I rushed outside and jumped back into the patrol car and sped off back up to the estate.

It was dark now so I drove the car back and forth along the avenue where the cows had been last reported by that elderly lady and with my headlights on full beam drove past her house several times in both directions.

My suspicion was confirmed by doing this. The beam from our headlight did not shine onto her window. There was no road where a passing car would travel that would do as she described.

So what was that bright light that we had both assumed to be car headlights that had grown suddenly in brilliance and seemingly caused the cows to instantly disappear?

And was it the same light later 'beamed' onto me?

I slept well when I returned home after that night shift and in the morning woke up with a new vigour. There were two days off work for me to relax and try to put this whole affair into some sort of context. So - after having a late brunch - I made my way to the vegetable patch at the bottom of the garden. I liked spending time here and even in late autumn there was always plenty to do so it was a great place to think - and I certainly had lots to think about.

One thing that I decided I must now consider was to seek medical advice on that irritating itchy mark on my left foot as it was getting worse and no amount of bathing or lotions seemed to be working. So I made an appointment at the doctors for the following day.

After tea, I settled down to relax for an evening in front of the TV when 'Our kid' - my eldest brother Colin - called and what he was about to tell me made the hairs on the back of my neck stand up.

Colin worked for the local council as a groundkeeper at two of the schools in the area, Todmorden High School and Ferney Lee Junior school. He had been talking to the caretaker at Ferney Lee - Leonard Smith - who by chance had previously been a special constable based at Todmorden for several years. We had even worked together on occasions.

Leonard was a stickler for detail and a no nonsense kind of person. He most definitely was not the sort to seek attention and led his life by the rules laid down. He would never bend those rules or attempt to hide from the truth. So I knew right away that what our kid just told me was another shot in the arm for my story. So I phoned Len up straight away and arranged a meeting.

At first Leonard was a bit shy about coming forward and wanted me to explain what I had witnessed myself as he had just heard whispers on the local grapevine but wanted to hear it from me directly before committing himself to telling others.

Having described my sighting the groundkeeper expressed great relief and told me what had occurred to him that same morning. After asking for my assurance that his name would not be mentioned in the public domain, to which I made a solemn promise until he much later did give consent, he felt reassured that what he was about to tell me would go no further.

We settled down in his office come store room at the school and he began to relate his own remarkable tale about his encounter with what must have been the same thing that I had seen at closer quarters.

At about five fifteen in the morning of that same day – 29 November - Leonard had been walking across the school yard towards the boiler house to fire the heating system up for the building. At weekends when school was closed it was used for social functions. He did this every morning anyway during the winter months to keep the building properly aired. But as he was doing this task on that early Saturday he found himself looking up at the dark sky and smiling because the heavy rain had stopped.

Then, suddenly he 'froze to the spot', as he put it.

'*I could not believe my eyes*' he told me – '*because rising slowly from the valley below was a large sphere like object*'.

This was coming up from Burnley Road - just where I was then parked - out of sight and unbeknown to Len. He told me that the object kept rising to just under the low cloud cover as he stood outside the school rooted to the spot. It then made 'Zig Zag' movements from one side of the valley to the other and shot off 'like a bullet' – heading north west towards Burnley.

Len added that there was no noise at all despite the morning being quiet and he being in the open but this incident had really scared him. I knew that he was not the kind of bloke to scare easily so I think he was really just uneasy at not being able to explain what he was watching, rather than frightened for his own safety.

I was relieved to discover part of my story that I had missed during my 'reality blink' after that huge flash of light - describing how the object I had seen low down had actually disappeared from view by flying upward. But rather more importantly, I now knew for sure that what I had witnessed actually had happened.

As I left Leonard Smith in the school there was a new spring in my step. It remained over the next couple of days as I relaxed at home. So by the time I visited Dr Williams about the mark on my foot I was more settled. He examined the itchy patch and thought it was nothing to worry about. After prescribing an ointment he told me that it should clear up in a few days, suggesting a form of psoriasis - a condition that I had never suffered with before or since. He did add that such a mark could have been brought on as a result of a severe shock to the system, but usually you would expect a larger part of the body to have been affected.

Returning to work on Wednesday 3 December 1980 I was thankfully off nights and now on the afternoon shift. I was also full of myself. I just wanted to tell everybody about what Leonard had seen, but could not because of my promise to him.

However, there was a message waiting in my 'tray' from a local reporter - Jeff Hanson from the regional covering the Calder Valley. He wanted to interview me. 'Somebody' had evidently contacted the press.

I did not mind giving him an interview as long as it was okay with my senior officers. So arrangements were made and I had my photograph taken to accompany his piece. Frankly I treated it as a bit of a laugh as me being in the papers seemed daft. I thought it could do no harm.

Having no experience of dealing with the media at that point I spoke freely unaware that papers pick up on little things they think will make for a good story.

So I described to the reporter a vague feeling that I had sensed whilst watching the object at very close quarters. It had been bugging me for days and was most odd – rather like a voice talking *inside* my head that just seemed to say to me - '*this is not for your eyes, Godfrey. You should* ***not*** *be seeing this.*'

As a result my increasingly 'weird' close encounter went into the *Hebden Bridge Times* on Friday 5 December 1980 headed: - '*May the force be with* you' – an ironic reference to that recent Star Wars movie. The sub heading was '*Amazing encounter in Calder Valley*'. My story was alongside that of the Halifax officers atop the front page together with an unflattering photo of me.

On seeing this in black and white I had that feeling you get after you express your mind but wish you had said nothing. I have long wondered where my life would have led if I had just declined that interview. Would these events have faded into obscurity never to even reach Jenny's UFO group over in Manchester?

But it was too late to worry about any of that now, because there was no hiding place after the press had become involved.

It soon felt like not just the people of Todmorden but the entire world wanted to know what I had seen.

CHAPTER FIVE

Hypnosis.... What's That All About?

Soon after my story appeared in the local paper I was called into the Inspectors office and informed that I was now to become community constable for the village of Walsden.

At any other time I would have been delighted about being chosen for that position but a good friend of mine - PC Phillip Walmsley – was already doing a fine job in this small village a mile or two south of Todmorden and he was well liked and respected by those who lived there.

It felt like the powers that be just wanted me out of the front line given my new found notoriety and that I was being 'put to grass' where I could not get into much trouble. 'Phil' was not pleased to be moved from Walsden either as he lived there which put him in a great position to police the moorside farms and riding stables day or night. Fellow villagers knew he was easy to contact and could call on him quickly in time of need.

For me it was different - I lived north of Todmorden and up the Burnley valley road So I was several miles away from the residents of Walsden who could not so easily reach me at a moment's notice in the same way as they could depend on 'Phil'. So this switch inconvenienced everybody.

Of course, there is always a bureaucratic reason behind a move like this and I felt that I knew only too well what it was here. Unfortunately, little did they know – but, if they were trying to get me out of the way of 'flying saucers' they could not have chosen a worse place - which I would discover only when my experience on Burnley Road reached the UFO research team from Manchester via that local paper and they decided to investigate.

One of that team was Jenny Randles who worked with me to write this book. She took a special interest in my story back then, being born locally and knowing Tod from visiting family during childhood. Her cousin lived here and was her regular childhood babysitter but was also now married to one of my sergeants at Todmorden who helped me face some of my problems. He was one of the good guys and she was told that she could trust me. So Jenny and several colleagues were on the case.

Jenny knew that the valleys around Walsden had produced UFO sightings in numbers before and after we met she told me of a strange event that occurred almost exactly two years before my own adventure in a place I was about to come to know well.

The witness was a young woman (by chance also called Jenny) who worked as a carer at a local children's home. At night she often visited one of the stables on the hills above Walsden village to see the horses and to take her sprightly dog for a walk. Jay (as I will call this witness to avoid confusion) took Jenny up the steep pathways to reveal what happened in that lonely spot.

Between September and November 1978 on these journeys she had seen several unusual ‘lightshows’ in the sky above the valley. During this period – like most local women – Jay was being particularly vigilant of what was happening when walking alone because of the terrifying crimes of the Yorkshire Ripper that - until finally apprehended in 1981 - were claiming innocent lives across parts of Yorkshire and Lancashire.

Intriguingly, Jay’s most spectacular sighting had been on the evening of 28 November – two years exactly before the night of my encounter. As she walked down the track from the stables into Walsden the woman was alerted by her dog – which stopped sniffing the hedgerows and looked bolt upright at the sky.

This sketch from artist Roy Sandbach, who came with Jenny Randles to the village to meet Jay shows the object she observed.

Following her pet’s gaze the woman saw a large oval mass with dark blobs or windows on the underside hovering very low overhead.

It was hanging there in total silence but the whole thing was surrounded by an eerie glow in the form of a silvery green mist.

Jay told Jenny Randles what it felt like to suddenly come face to face with this extraordinary object:

'*Imagine walking over the moors and suddenly seeing the QE II cruise liner in the sky overhead. You know it cannot* ***really*** *be up there – yet you are seeing it and so somehow it must be.*'

As she and her trusty companion stared up into the belly of this amazing beast the witness felt a sense of 'communion' between herself and the UFO. There was a tingling energy coming from it, buzzing the air, itching her skin with a hidden communication from the object.

'*Like we were joined at the soul,*' Jay poetically described it to Jenny.

It then vanished in a strange way: '*The thing split into two – repelling each other like poles of a magnet.*'

'*There were showers of sparks like electricity from a live wire as it broke apart....One part went south towards Manchester, the other over the moors towards Bacup. Then it was gone and I stood there and I cried. I felt like I had just lost my dearest friend.*'

This dramatic reaction to a close encounter is not at all unusual, Jenny tells me. If you suddenly come face to face with something that is completely impossible yet clearly real it shatters your entire view of the universe in an instant. Afterwards you feel emotionally drained.

Moreover this woman believed that this UFO had 'spoken to her' – but without actually hearing a voice coming out of it. Instead it was like something *'tickling my mind'* that '*used my thoughts and images to give me* a *message*' She added: -'*It was less a voice and more a 'knowing...I kept seeing or hearing the words* ***Do Not Be Afraid****. And I did not feel afraid.*'

I could very easily understand that weird aspect of this story, of course, because much the same thing had happened to me. Jenny told me that this woman had been very honest about this 'impossible' encounter and said that – if asked – she now realizes that she would have walked towards it across that hillside path 'like a lamb' responding on instinct regardless of danger.

She used analogies such as being plugged into a computer terminal and 'drained' of all emotional experience – and of seeing her life flash through her mind. And added that the whole thing was so profound it almost felt like an epiphany.

'*For many hours afterwards I was in a heightened state of emotion. I just could not think normally. Those few moments changed my life.*' She told Jenny.

Jenny asked this witness why she did not visit the police station in Tod and report what happened – quite possibly if she had done so to be greeted by a hopefully friendly but utterly befuddled desk officer.

Which in 1978 would, of course, have been a pre close encounter me! Jay had smiled and said it would have been 'futile'.

'*You had to have been there and seen that it was real in order to believe it had happened. Otherwise it will just seem absurd to anyone else. I* ***know*** *what happened but I cannot possibly expect everyone else who was not there to take my word for it. It is so very frustrating to be in this position.*'

Of course, when Jenny Randles told me of this case it rang so many bells in so many ways that I could really empathise with the plight of this woman. I faced the same situation two years later just three miles down the valley. In the end Jay was driven to leave and head south perhaps hoping to escape the memory of these events.

Happily oblivious to this recent history connecting close encounters and my new posting at Walsden I got on with my role there and started to enjoy working in the village. The job was totally different from policing in the town centre and the people were very friendly.

The part I enjoyed the most was the hospitality of the local landlords of the village pubs. They made me very welcome especially on cold winter nights with open fires in their grates crackling away warming the soul and the refreshment of a hardy drink went down very well!

Many a time I would walk into one of the pubs and place my helmet on the bar where a stool would find its way to me so I could rest my weary legs, light up a cigarette and consume a grand old pint of thick black 'Dark Mild'. I could then spend time talking to people around the bar and finding out things that otherwise may never have learnt about, if you get my drift.

Of course, this method of policing is no longer the 'done thing' – which is a pity because you become part of the community and people appreciate that. As 'one of them' they will trust you and tell you anything.

The long winter of 1980/81 passed and I had not been working in Walsden long when I was summoned into the station in Todmorden and met by yet another new Inspector who had transferred from Brighouse.

He lead me out into the yard at the back of the building and pointed towards a small contraption – a police pedal cycle. It had what we used to call 'sit up and beg' handlebars with a very heavy black/dark blue frame, three gears and solid tyres. This magnificent piece of machinery was complete with a shiny bell.

For a brief moment I thought this was a joke and chuckled: "*If you think I'm going to ride around on that thing you are a penny short of a shilling*."

When clear he was serious my second sentence was succinct – just two words and the second one was "off ".

Once I understood that this was really meant to be my transport instead of a patrol car I briefly imagined how the bike might unhappily 'go missing' in some mishap or other. But I realized that this would create a lot of paper work and I didn't fancy that!

No the best thing was to walk along with it and leave it in the back yard of my younger brother Stuart's house who lived in Walsden. I could then catch the bus home. 'That's what I'll do' I said to myself.

The Inspector seemed to take great satisfaction at

the thought of me riding this thing every day – which all at the station knew would be very uncomfortable given my hospitalization for those serious injuries to my nether regions in the 'line of duty'. So when I said that I could not ride for this reason, he became indignant and a little zealous in insisting he see me astride the frame.

At one point I informed him that if I could watch him ride it through 'Tod' on market day getting the respect of the crowds then I would ride it on my tour of duty as an equally authoritative figure before the locals.

I thought this was only fair, but he went into a kind of 'how dare you speak to me like that' stare and just marched off.

Little did I know at the time that this Inspector would cause me serious grief further down the line. This bike fiasco was merely the starting point of a vendetta.

A short while later I was in the village pub - making enquiries - when someone came in and said that a few local teenagers were now riding my police bike all around the village. Everybody stared at me to see my reaction. But I just shrugged at the news and carried on with another sip of those 'enquiries' whilst smiling:

"*Yeah, I told them that they could have a go on it, but to look after it as I didn't want it getting nicked whilst I was in here.*"

As for that bike - it became an increasing focus of confrontation between me and that Inspector. It got to a point that he became obsessed with it and made it his mission in life to catch me walking alongside the machine instead of riding full pelt on the saddle in pain to do so as he knew I would be. It was really quite sad.

Over and over I patiently explained about how the damage to my groin inflicted apprehending that assailant meant that I could not sit on the saddle for long. But he just seemed to get pleasure from ignoring medical reality and inflicting torture onto me. So in the end I put in an official complaint and he did seem to stop after that.

Of course, the downside was that I knew he would now be watching my every move and likely not hesitate to cause trouble given the slightest opportunity.

Things came to a head on the Easter bank holiday in 1981 whilst I was sorting out the traffic congestion outside Gordon Riggs Garden Centre in Walsden. It was chaos in those days as there were no regulations in place and motorists could park anywhere they fancied.

I received a radio message to return to the police station and meet with my nemesis and thought to myself grimly - 'what does he want now?'

So I informed control that I was up to my eyes with traffic problems - but the Inspector insisted that I return immediately into town and off back to the station I went.

I was not happy to have to stop this necessary job.

When I arrived at the station the inspector duly informed me that he had travelled over from Sowerby Bridge and on his way passed a car parked in a very dangerous position on a bend that had double yellow lines. This was at Cinder Hill on Halifax Road. He went on to tell me to go straight to this location and find and then interview the driver and report him for that offence.

What annoyed me was the thin smile on his face as he did this. I just looked at him with a blank stare and when he asked me what was up I had to tell him. It was one of those mad moments that you get sometimes and you just let rip and to hell with the consequences.

My words as I remember went something like:

"*You have brought me down from Walsden where I was sorting out serious traffic problems, to go to Cinder Hill and book a motorist for an offence that you deemed dangerous yet drove straight past and did nothing about yourself? If it was that bloody dangerous why did you not sort it there and then*?"

I turned round and left the room half expecting him to call me back - then returned to Walsden seething over him putting safety behind his war with me.

My duties in Walsden did now seem to get shorter and shorter. So for weeks I was being taken back to work in Todmorden. 'Because we are short staffed' was the usual reason given when I asked why. Yet I could see that the same number of bobbies were still working as before I had been moved to Walsden.

So naturally I suspected that there was another reason and did not need two guesses as to who might be behind the alterations.

Gradually I came to believe that I was being victimized after the events in the final few months of the previous year – starting with the Adamski death in June and my UFO encounter on Burnley Road in November. The local revelations and chatter in public about all of this were for some reason not sitting well with factions within the West Yorkshire constabulary. Had I trodden inadvertently on toes trying to be honest and helpful?

I tried to ignore this inspector and just get on with my work, making trips back to Walsden whenever duties allowed as the village deserved a local copper. Of course, I had expected a bit of ribbing from the public after the local paper came out, but to my surprise it never really came from those outside the police. In fact people on the streets were coming up to me and recounting their own sightings instead and there was an awful lot of them from people in all different walks of life.

One particular report came to me from a colleague at the station. This had occurred at Sharneyford on the road to Bacup over moors that crossed the border. There were two police officers on patrol in a vehicle that night up on the tops in the early hours of 27 October 1967.

I shall call them 'Eddy' and 'Sid'. They had parked their car on the Todmorden side of the county waiting for a disqualified driver who they had been advised was ignoring the ban and still driving every morning from Bacup to the pipe works situated on Bacup Road in Tod.

'Sid' was rolling a cigarette whilst 'Eddy' was watching the road for the appearance of this illegal driver, when over the crest of the hill in front of them and well below the cloud ceiling a bright light was seen that resolved into a large cone shaped object. It moved side to side and then headed towards them.

The object now stopped for a moment and then

passed over the road and slowly down the valley between their car and Stoodley Pike – a hilltop monument just outside town.

Instead of waiting for the disqualified driver the two officers pursued the object as far as possible before it changed direction again and went over the moors toward Gorply Waterworks where they lost sight.

The two startled policemen reported these events to the night duty inspector back at Todmorden and he called the 'War Office' at the Ministry of Defence in London. The inspector was advised by them to file a report – which they all did – but there was no further response on the matter from Whitehall.

However, this incident was independently corroborated by Lancashire Police officers just over the border about two miles from my colleagues. This was at Bacup police station – in fact the building used by the BBC during the early 1980s as the fictional police station for their drama 'Juliet Bravo'. Brian Earnshaw - a police officer here - had heard radio interference crackling on the shortwave communication with local bobbies and gone outside in search of the cause. He saw about 250 feet above the building a 'cigar' shaped object with what looked like windows on the side. It gave off a bright glow and made a 'whirring' noise.

Two other local officers reported the object at the same time and watched it climb up and disappear. An official report was filed and Lancashire police headquarters became dismissive of the whole thing – even at one point trying to kill interest from the media by saying it was just a hoax that got out of hand.

The PCs involved denied this and insisted their report was the truth and Bacup police backed them locally saying that there was 'no reasonable explanation' for what was described. Although sceptics did point out that there had been several sightings that week by police patrols in Devon of what they called a 'flying cross' which research later revealed were probably caused by the planet Venus being very bright in the night sky.

Of course, the independent report from my friend and his colleague at Todmorden must cast this sighting in another light and suggests it was much more interesting than the Lancashire Constabulary were keen for it to be considered. Probably thanks to the negative comments about the police in Devon.

It seems as if police procedures on both sides of the border were well aligned and the downplaying anything to do with flying saucers began long before my report.

I could certainly see parallels with what was happening to me 14 years later. Perhaps UFOs and the need for perceived respect within the police are difficult to reconcile. But the truth should never be suppressed or someone be mistreated *because* they report that truth.

This same location – those moors around Sharneyford – has been host to further sightings since 1967. Jenny Randles tells of one case that happened here almost on the same spot beside the county border.

The witness - 'Angela' - was driving from Bacup to Todmorden late at night on 4 February 1988 when she spotted a strange egg shaped object over the moors. Angela worked in a science lab and so was fascinated by the internal features she saw within the object:

'*Like a swirling liquid or fire embers with constantly changing patterns,*' she described this composition in her report to Jenny.

There have been so many witnesses to odd things in this area it has been dubbed 'UFO alley' by locals – and others have described the same effect seen here where the innards of an object move like 'wriggling worms'.

These are just a few of many encounters in and around Todmorden and I was being informed of more on almost a daily basis with no reason to disbelieve any of them. How could I given what had just happened to me?

I did wonder at the time why the sightings were rarely getting reported publicly, but of course many of these witnesses had no idea who to contact or had not wanted to be ridiculed. So I suppose I had become someone who they felt they could now trust because we shared that ineffable bond of seeing the impossible.

Several of these puzzled witnesses even suggested that we start-up a UFO group in Todmorden and so we did - meeting at different pubs and social clubs to discuss one another's experiences as the numbers grew. I enjoyed those get-togethers.

It was during this time that I got a very intriguing phone call at work from the Fraud Squad of the Greater Manchester Police . This was certainly not something I was used to. It was a Detective Inspector called Norman Collinson.

Rather startled I returned his call and arranged to meet him. It all sounded very 'hush hush' and I was wondering why a DCI and big player in the Fraud Squad from a neighbouring force wanted to meet me. He had chosen not to discuss his reasons on the phone.

After giving him my number he later called me at home and informed that it was to do with my UFO encounter and would it be possible to obtain a filmed interview. It took some thought and gentle persuasion but I agreed and a date was set up. Norman asked me not to discuss what was happening with anyone at work.

This all made me feel a little uneasy and I was unsure why it was all being handled secretively, but he did mention the name Adamski in connection with my sighting and that started to ring alarm bells. To be aware of both events and connecting them as if they were linked was a real cause for me to worry.

It was to be late Spring of 1981 before I got to meet DCI Collinson and he arrived with three other people.

Harry Harris said he was a solicitor with a practice in south Manchester, Mike Sacks was a local 1960s pop group musician who now worked as a tailor in Jenny's home village of Stacksteads near Bacup, and Gerry Mitchell – an insurance broker – who had been a bomber pilot and pathfinder during the second world war.

This was a rather strange combination of individuals I thought. It turned out that they all simply shared an interest in UFO's, mostly through direct experience - which was reassuring given my initial thoughts about a fraud inspector and solicitor wanting to come talk to me which had briefly made me double check that I had not accidentally made an error in my expenses at work!

We sat down and over a nice cup of tea and I recounted what I had seen on that night four or five months earlier and then we moved onto the 'Adamski' affair. It was all perfectly amicable and very thorough.

A little later - when I met Jenny Randles from that group – she explained that they all belonged to a small team of UFO investigators that met regularly in Manchester to investigate major cases in the north. It had been operating since 1963 and was called MUFORA (Manchester UFO Research Association).Jenny had been a member since 1973 and Mike and Norman had joined in the past two years after reporting their own UFO experiences to the group. Harry was a more recent recruit with his own special project. MUFORA had read about both the Adamski case and my encounter in the local press and Jenny knew of me via her cousin so it was decided it was worth finding out further details.

Former RAF pilot Gerry Mitchell had a UFO sighting in May 1977 whilst driving near sunset through open country at Lymm in Cheshire. He was suddenly gripped by an overwhelming belief that something was about to happen – so powerful that he drove onto the side of the road, stopped and wound down the window awaiting the inevitable.

By now it was so intense he just sat there whilst noticing that all ambient sounds had disappeared and time seemed to have slowed down almost to a halt. Then a formation of three green spheres whizzed past the side of the car and disappeared. Gerry 'came to' as if emerging from a trance and realized the enormity of what had just happened to him.

Jenny explained that this strange state of dissociated consciousness is often reported by a witness to a close encounter and coined a term for it – the 'Oz Factor'.

'I called it this because it feels as if the witness is temporarily extracted from our world to visit another 'reality' where rules of time and space seem different - just like Dorothy suddenly arrives in Oz in the classic fairy tale after encountering a force arriving from the sky and has no idea how or why.'

Her term is used in UFO research and Jenny notes that US rock band – Unwritten Law – titled their second studio album after it – with lyrics that seem to allude to the weird state of detachment during a close encounter.

DCI Norman Collinson's sighting that took him to MUFORA had occurred on 2 April 1976 after finishing a shift in Salford. It was 1.50 am and he was on the M66 motorway at Heywood near Rochdale in the Lancashire Pennines when he saw a strange light in the west. At first he assumed it was military air traffic as it had one single bright light – not flashing navigation beacons like a civil aircraft - so paid attention only out of curiosity at first.

Then it came closer and passed across his view, revealing itself as a large disc about a quarter the size of the full moon. This was before helicopters were often used at night so he was sure it was some kind of military operation. He took his usual turn into Heywood to go home, losing the object in streetlights. But as he reached a darker stretch of road he saw the object again – now moving very slowly eastwards (towards Walsden).

By now Norman was intrigued and stopped his car and got out. Everywhere was quiet and the large disc moved in a series of 'box' like patterns. It then headed over the rooftops of Heywood.

Determined to give chase, the DCI jumped back in his car catching the object several hundred yards away. He leapt out again as the disc moved around above his head, desperately looking for another witness to back him up, but nobody was about in the deserted community as it was now after 2 am.

Suddenly the disc accelerated eastwards at phenomenal speed and disappeared over the hills in just a couple of seconds, dispelling any thought that this could just be a military aircraft.

Being a trained investigative officer the DCI reported what had happened to the MoD in London, who sent him a reply basically saying they would keep it on file but did not have the resources to dig into what it was. So he phoned Manchester Airport to see if they had any explanation. They were friendly and helpful and offered to back him up at the MoD and would get back to him if they could find an answer. They never did.

In the end Norman Collinson found his way to MUFORA almost as a last resort (like people in the street were doing with me) because nobody in authority seemed interested in following up what he had seen that night. He became intrigued and joined the small select band that was purposefully kept to about 10 UFO researchers with varied interests to retain confidentiality.

Mike Sacks made records in the 1960s as part of group Mike Sax and The Idols and still puts music on the net today. He had a sighting of an orange ball of fire moving slowly over the hills in October 1978 that caused him to report the sighting to Jodrell Bank science centre, who in turn, suggested he contact Jenny Randles.

Having her phone number from that event Mike was later in a position to call her directly at about 2 am on 24 February 1979 to say that he had just watched an even more spectacular UFO from his bedroom window where he had been looking after his young son who was poorly with tonsillitis.

The bedroom had filled with pulsing light and both he and his wife had watched whilst an orange ball of fire hovered in the south over a small quarry. When over the top of this outcrop it stopped dead in an amazingly impossible motion, lit up the ground below and now revealed itself as an arc of bluish light with three rings below that pulsed in a deep amber hue. Moments before he called Jenny the UFO sank above the quarry and disappeared.

After reporting what had occurred Mike told Jenny he was heading up to the quarry to see if the UFO had now landed. He first drove to pick up his brother who had a camera and they walked up moors to the location. Back at home Mike's wife and stricken son had kept watching through the window hoping to see if the UFO 'took off'. But they never saw it again.

Reaching the quarry the Sacks brothers saw nothing further – other than a row of lights that Mike says he walked towards as a voice in his head kept telling him the word 'portakabin' – implying that this small hut for quarry workers was all that they were viewing.

Yet next morning in daylight back in the quarry they discovered there was no structure like this present!

Here is how Mike was to draw the UFO that he saw fall from the sky above Stack-steads.

Note how in so many of these cases – my own included – there is reference to this 'voice' in the mind talking to the witness. Jenny tells me it is very much a key to understanding what is happening because it is so frequently reported during close encounters. A few witnesses say it sounds like the voice they hear in their heads when talking to themselves. She thinks this a clue.

Despite seeing nothing further on the hilltops above Stacksteads after calling Jenny the Sacks brothers bumped into two police constables from the station at Bacup who had just seen an orange ball of light silently streak across the valley from the road below. Their sighting was at about 2.35 am - half an hour after Mike Sacks had already phoned Jenny. The PCs watched it disappear towards the quarry and went up to investigate even though - when Norman Collinson interviewed them a few days later - they could not really explain why they walked up there in the pitch dark because they had never thought the UFO was going to land. It was moving fast across the sky heading westward.

Mike and his brother had somehow missed this second UFO - despite them then both then being on the open hillside with full view of the skyline and immediately above the location of these police officers. But they were being distracted by that voice in the head saying 'portakabin'.

Frustratingly, Jenny was unable to do anything immediately about Mike's call. She then lived miles from Bacup and was giving a lecture at Cheshire libraries in Crewe next day so was booked on an early train. Norman Collinson went out to do initial investigation and managed to get the police officers to talk to him, though they chose not to go public with their story after he did and never filed a written report.

Later Jenny was able to dig deep into this case which revealed remarkable details. There were in fact other independent sightings of this event across Lancashire that night. Security police at an MoD depot near Blackburn filed a report to be kept secret by the Ministry for 30 years until it was released under the Freedom of Information Act recently. It explained how they watched the same object zoom across the sky.

A security guard on the pier at Blackpool told Jenny how the girders shook as a ball of orange fire disappeared toward the west, after which lights spiraled from beneath the Irish Sea and headed into the sky.

Events of that night were even debated in parliament because residents of a caravan park near Scarisbrick were shaken out of bed by what looks to be the same roaring orange ball seen over Blackpool and possibly witnessed by the police at Stacksteads. The local Ormskirk MP (later a TV chat show host) Robert Kilroy Silk thought this could be a military aircraft breaking low flying rules in controlled airspace and was told that a 'special exercise' was underway involving US F-111 jets - though not what the jets were 'chasing' which we might suspect was the UFO that Mike watched shortly before. Jenny asked the USAF in writing if this was true and they withdrew their claim that they were ever involved in any part of the sightings that night!

This remarkable collection of UFO sightings was spread around the Pennines. It was so strange that I could see we needed those meetings in Todmorden to act as a focus for other disenfranchised witnesses who were surely out there waiting to find somebody to talk to.

MUFORA had chosen just to investigate and document the evidence without public profile as we saw earlier. Doing things discretely gave them connections at places such as the Universities in Manchester where friendly scientists would look for hard evidence and the Kodak laboratories in Hemel Hempstead who let them visit to analyse photographic cases. Plus the science centre at Jodrell Bank quietly assisted on some cases reciprocating those lectures in the planetarium by Jenny. In one case helping solve a case as a mirage of stars.

I could understand why scientists were afraid of being openly linked with UFOs as it was rather like the witnesses that approached me being afraid of how others would treat them. As I was finding out within the force your reputation can take a nosedive the moment you reveal what has happened before your eyes. Yet UFOs are so fascinating people need answers so they seek help.

Harry Harris – the latest MUFORA recruit - had access to specialist video recording equipment which he used to build a personal archive of witness testimony. As a lawyer he hoped to persuade someone in authority that there was enough serious evidence of UFO reality with this filmed record that open public hearings and a national enquiry would follow. It was a laudable aim.

So it was to these people that I now told my story in front of Harry's video camera as I answered all DCI Collinson's questions.

At times I thought I was being grilled as a suspect in a major crime rather than having a gentle 'chat' with a colleague. Norman really went to town and he had a particular attention for detail that came with his job. Indeed it was this 'pickiness' that first led us to realise that there seemed to be a period of 'missing time' involved in my close encounter. That revelation would be another turning point that would change my life.

We went over and over the details of that night from me heading onto Burnley Road at 5.10 am and returning there later to pick up Malcolm Agley and go back to the scene. Malcolm confirmed this was just before 6 am when his shift ended and that time check created a puzzle that I had not immediately noticed but explained his initial reluctance to get into my patrol car.

Given these facts we suspected that a period of time was absent from my conscious memory on Burnley Road. The whole sequence from driving away to returning with PC Agley should not have taken more than fifteen minutes. So why had it lasted half an hour longer than this?

This discovery by DCI Collinson left me intrigued and so I discussed it with some of the local UFO club members at our next meeting. I was informed by one of them that there were other cases of people who had seen a UFO and could not account for 'missing time'. Indeed I was given a book to read by one of the members about such an incident. It told of a couple called Betty and Barney Hill in America who had claimed that they had recovered a memory during a similar gap in time that emerged after they saw a UFO over a highway in New England. That memory implied that they had been abducted into the UFO by aliens and that recall at first suppressed by their minds.

At the time I thought it was all rather 'Doctor Who' and far-fetched. But if people genuinely believed that they had been abducted, who was I to judge their story given what others were doubtless thinking about me but that I knew really had happened.

Certainly this possibility got me wondering about just what might have occurred during that period between seeing the bright light flash in my eyes and 'coming to' driving a further along down Burnley Road. Why was a chunk of my memory simply not there when I must have started the car and driven that distance?

After this disturbing first brush with the possibility that something was lurking inside my head removed from my recall, DCI Collinson contacted me again in early Summer 1981 and informed me that there had been some discussion amongst the UFO team about what to do next. Harry Harris had suggested that they try 'Hypnotic Regression'.

I was assured that this method had been used in cases in the US and might be able to release the memory that seemed to be blocked by my mind.

'Would I be willing?' Norman asked and I told him honestly that I needed time to think over such a serious request and was not even sure what hypnotic regression meant.

In the end I told the DCI that I would think about his suggestion, which I did long and hard over the next couple of weeks. My desire to resolve why I had this chunk of missing time was too strong to resist.

So when DCI Collinson next called me to say that Harry Harris had found two psychiatrists who were willing to hypnotise and 'regress' me and – crucially – that they had no idea what the subject matter would be about or even of one another's involvement in this investigation - then I agreed to go ahead.

Harry preferred them to be ignorant of my story because he wanted these two doctors to approach the matter without any expectations of what they might be looking for. This made sense to me – so all that these two doctors were told was that I was a policeman and that there would be a DCI present and also a solicitor. They would then try to take me back to an incident that had occurred on the 28/29th November the previous year during my patrol.

The two doctors had both agreed to try and I could see right away that uncovering a UFO encounter would be the very last thing likely to be on their minds. They both later said they assumed it was to do with a crime that I had been involved in policing and for which added details might help its resolution.

One of the psychatrists was a Professor Robert Blair who had worked at Springfield Hospital in Bury and was now a lecturer at Manchester University. The other was a Dr Joseph Jaffee who was a physician with a private practice on the posh John Street in central Manchester (the northern equivalent of London's Harley Street). He did work for the Greater Manchester Police with victims of violent assaults such as rape cases and other traumatic crimes hoping to find missing details they had repressed and that might help track down the assailant. A few months after working with me he became Lord Mayor for the City of Salford.

I talked to Jenny Randles in the weeks before these sessions when she came to Tod and began recording details like the damage to my police boot. Jenny told me she had serious reservations about the use of regression hypnosis in UFO cases and would not personally get involved in that side of the case, but asked me what I was expecting. So I told her that I had been 'flummoxed' by my encounter and just wanted to prove to myself and others that it was real and not an hallucination. I hoped that the hypnosis would let me recall the experience more clearly and resolve any confusion I had. I was not expecting it to reveal new things that I had no memory about at all.

On Sunday 2 August 1981 I drove down the motorway heading towards Manchester for the first session. This would be with Professor Blair as he had no prior interest in UFOs which the researchers considered a plus. My mind was all over the place and I was unsure what to expect. 'Would I be able to be hypnotised?' and 'What would it be like?' These questions never stopped and when I reached my destination I had 'butterflies'.

Harry and the DCI were waiting for me alongside Mike Sacks. Harry had his camcorder with him and asked me if I minded if he filmed the session. I agreed because at the time I thought it would be a good idea to prove what had happened afterward. This was getting quite scary, but I did not know why. This session was at Professor Blair's large Victorian property in north Manchester with grand entrance hall and large open staircase leading off to the first floor. Professor Blair was as I imagined him in every sense.

With the greatest respect he fitted my idea of an eccentric professor to a tee. Blair spoke with obvious authority but there was a kindness in his voice. He also had a warm handshake and made me feel welcome and relaxed. Harry enquired about recording the session on film, but to his huge disappointment the Professor refused. I remember looking back at the three of them as I climbed the stairs, it was a sorry sight as they looked like three little boys who had found a penny but had lost a pound. They were gutted!

Entering the consulting room I remember feeling cold and a shivering sensation came over me – just like the saying 'Somebody walking over your grave'. Yet it was a warm summer's evening. The room was sparse and uninviting with, on one side, a rather old looking settee and a white sink next to it. There was also a large desk and a well-worn high backed armchair.

The Professor talked me through what was going to happen and asked if I consented to be hypnotised, although he did say that he could never promise that it would work as sometimes a subject just could not be 'put under'. I gave him the go ahead and I was seated on this consulting bench - sat upright and not lying down as I had half expected in a psychiatrist's office. So I just made myself as comfortable as I could.

I was surprised when Dr Blair just sat there talking to me in a soft, quiet and yet persistently droning voice. My head filled with ideas from the cinema I had been expecting a pocket watch swinging from side to side or a ticking metronome, but it was nothing like that. The voice seemed to get further and further away as he spoke on - until it became inaudible and I opened my eyes because I had this thumping headache. So I think I said something like:- *'I'm sorry I cannot seem to drop off I have got a stinking head'.*

Professor Blair just smiled and led me back downstairs whilst I felt as if I had let everyone down by not being 'susceptible'. Indeed, it was only when he started telling Harry and the others that the session had been a success that I even realised that I *had* been hypnotized. Almost an hour had evidently passed between my losing touch with his voice and then sitting up! During this period I had described my UFO event and the doctor said he found it unbelievable but he was certain that something really had happened to me on that night and he could not explain it.

Because I had become very distressed during the session and complained of sharp pains in my head when he questioned this, he had decided to bring me out of hypnosis and ask my subconscious to '*forget*' all memory to lower any trauma - hence my amnesia.

When we left the Professors house, there were questions coming from all directions out of the investigators around me - but I could not answer any of them. I was as much in the dark as they were and felt terrible to be so unhelpful but I simply did not recall anything that I may have said whilst under hypnosis. In any case this headache was really now thumping and getting me down. So I bid them goodnight and set off home. It was a long drive and the car headlights were piercing my eyes and making my head throb so I called into a motorway service station for a rest to recover.

Pulling up in the car park I was nauseous and made my way to the washroom and just made it into a cubicle before I violently threw up. By now I felt really rough and the headache was splitting. I had bought some aspirin at the convenience store on site and went for a brew in the cafe swallowing three of them in one go before I lit a cigarette up and sat there feeling dog rough.

'What the hell was up with me?' I thought. Taking in deep breaths I started to sweat and the room I was seated in span around with the sound of other customers getting louder and louder. I just about managed to struggle outside into the cooler night air.

Gradually I inched my way back toward the car but my legs felt like lumps of lead with a life of their own and just not interested in doing what I was instructing them to do. I could sense that people around me were looking concerned or maybe suspecting that I was drunk. But I recall little after that, only waking up on the back seat of my car curled up and it was many hours later and broad daylight.

Whilst I had a very dry throat my headache was gone. I just wanted to get home and set off without bothering to quench my thirst. Pulling up outside my house I was worrying about what was going on in there. I could see that the curtains were still drawn and a quick glance at my watch told me that it was 6.30 am and everybody was still in bed. So I unlocked the door and made my way to the kitchen and put the kettle on.

As I waited for the water to boil I lit a cigarette and opened the back door which led out into the garden at the rear of the house. I stood there taking in the fresh air and could hear the early morning bird calls. I stepped outside with a freshly brewed pot of tea and sat at the table on the raised patio situated at the top of the garden with a panoramic view of the valley towards Centre Vale Park. I could see below a couple of people walking their dogs and the sound of the milkman at the front of the house, delivering his wares. There is something special about the sound of clinking milk bottles in the early morning hours that is so peaceful and tells you all is well with the world.

I must have dropped off sat out there in those pleasant surroundings because the next thing I knew I was awake and feeling very strange. My headache had come back with a vengeance and my legs were heavy and I had started to sweat profusely again. All that I could do was crash out on top of the bed.

And then the 'dreams' started!

There was this strange noise all around me reverberating like an echo that was swirling about inside my head:- '*Minimm manimm menimm manumm*'.

It was all in weird tones hard to describe in words.

Then this image kept appearing in my mind and it was nothing like I had ever seen. The figure was about 3ft high with a very large light-bulb shaped head which looked far too big for the body underneath. There were also those eyes – large, black and egg shaped – they were really so very odd. But even stranger was that there was no mouth or trace of a nose on the face.

The being kept putting that face right up to mine and staring deep into my eyes and reaching out with what looked like withered arms sprouting long fingers trying to touch me. I just kept shouting really loud for it to get off me and lashing out with my fists, but it kept coming back again and again.

Finally I managed to get my foot into the flimsy body of this creature and with a mighty kick it fell to the ground and so did I, carried forward by the momentum of my lunge. I crashed to the floor with a bump.

In the waking world I had fallen out of bed.

I was glad to get back to work next day just to put this scary stuff aside. The lads seemed to be getting on with what needed to be done and I was about to go on patrol when an Inspector over from division called and asked to see me and I was rather puzzled!

"How is your little UFO group doing?" he asked me as I was about to sit down.

It was a most odd question from an outsider but I replied cheerfully: -

"Um, ok, sir, why do you ask?"

"Just interested, it's – what - six months or so since it was formed? I like to take an interest in what my officers get up to when they are off-duty and how they spend their leisure time"

I was shocked and thought 'what is going on here?

"Yes sir it will be about that long," I replied.

"Have you ever thought of taking your sergeants exam?" He then added out of the blue. Now I knew that something was going on.

"Not really sir, I like things as they are. I've got no ambitions."

"Well you should have some. We are always on the look-out for the right men to become sergeants."

Where was this suddenly coming from, I wondered?

He carried on the conversation asking me about who was in the group and where we held our meetings. What started out as a general discussion seemed to be turning into something of an inquisition. I felt rather uneasy by the end of it and that he was overstepping the mark by digging so deep into my private life.

I became rather vague with my answers to his constant questions after that point and I think he saw this and gave up.

"Who's that Inspector from Halifax then, I've never seen him before have you?" I asked 'Graham', one of our long serving officers when it was over.

'Graham' was the font of all knowledge within the force and what he did not know was hardly worth knowing as the saying goes.

" No idea - he's a new one on me, too, but I'll do a bit of ringing round" he replied with a wink and a gentle tapping of his finger to the side of his nose.

When I told him what the Inspector had asked he developed a broad grin that turned into a roaring laugh.

"You become a sergeant. As if. 'Looking for the right men' hah! I think he's travelled too far up the valley and the air has got to his brain!"

A little later I was just finishing off some paperwork when 'Graham' came into the parade room with a rather serious look on his face that told me something was up - a something that we all dread.

"Doctors here, he's reporting a suspected infant death, best come in and listen to what he has to say because you will be dealing with it."

My stomach turned over and I went through to the interview room and listened intently to the doctor.

"Sorry to put this onto your shoulders," he said somberly. *"But I have to go back with you. There is nothing suspicious about the death, tragic as it is, it is just the mother is struggling to accept that her child is gone."*

I discovered that this reaction was not unusual, but I gathered up the paperwork needed for a sudden death report and followed the Doctor. This was going to be very difficult for me to deal with as a family man.

No amount of training can prepare you for such a traumatic event. You are a human being inside that uniform but more importantly, how you deal with the aftermath of such a tragedy with so many life shattering emotions will leave a mark on the parents and they will remember your visit for the rest of their days.

On entering the room the mum was cradling the child in her arms and singing quietly whilst rocking gently from side to side. It brought a lump to my throat just watching her agony.

I smiled and sat down slowly onto the couch and glanced at the dad who was fighting to keep control of his own emotions.

The Doctor spoke very quietly and tried to explain why the police were present but mum just kept holding the infant tightly At this the doctor looked across the room at me and I knew it was down to me now to respond appropriately.

But before I could say anything dad took control and suggested mum go into the kitchen and make baby its bottle. Mum handed over the baby to dad on instinct and did as requested. Quickly but gently dad then passed the child across to me and I headed for the car whilst mum was out of the room to spare her further pain.

As I drove slowly away I felt utterly bereft. I desperately wanted to stop and go back and say it was all just a mistake, your child is fine, but knew that I could not. And that I was doing what had to be done for the good of everyone. But it was still one of my worst days of my career in the police.

It took me a long time to get over those events but I needed to find courage to return to that house and make sure that they were coping with the aftermath. Amazingly, I was made to feel welcome and was deeply impressed by how they handled these awful circumstances. This experience taught me a lot about human nature and how lucky we are not to have to go through an ordeal such as they did.

It was something like that which I needed to put all my far less terrible troubles into proper perspective. What seems like the end of the world to you at the time and from which nothing is ever going to get better can be seen for what it really is when you remember those people who have had their heart ripped open and torn from their chest. Everything else is really so small and insignificant by comparison.

It hardly seemed that long since my first hypnotic session with Professor Blair but over a month had gone by and Harry was back on the phone saying they had fixed the second session with the other psychiatrist - Dr Joseph Jaffee.

This time it was to be on Wednesday 9 September 1981 at his practice on John Street, just off Deansgate in Manchester city centre. Jaffee had agreed for the session to be video filmed by Harry so long as I consented. I was just as eager for this visual record as the others were because I wanted to know what I was saying and still had no memory at all of what happened during the first session.

Dr Jaffee's practice was a bit more 'up market' than Blair's. It was very modern with a receptionist and a nurse. We entered the consulting room and I remember that there was what looked like a black leather 'Dentist' chair. At the side of this was a machine which turned out to be a monitor for my heartbeat. It was a good job this was not strapped to me at that moment because my heart was racing with anticipation before we even started.

The room was kept in dim light and at a warm temperature even in Summer, which was part of the induction process I guess. Dr Jaffee himself was a grey haired gentleman who wore spectacles and dressed in a short white clinic coat that made him look very professional. When he spoke he used a soft gentle voice.

Having had it explained to him by DCI Collinson what was required and given only the time and date to which they wished him to regress me, Jaffee attached the heart monitor equipment to my wrists and chest area.

The video equipment was set up by Harry and the session started. But all I can remember was listening to the Doctors voice – before – once again - I 'woke up' and glanced at the large clock at the back of the room and an hour had gone by in a flash.

The look on everybody's face around me suggested that they were very excited at what happened during the session but when I asked what this was they would only say that the doctor had been forced to wake me up because I had become so distressed that the heart monitor shot off the scale with readings like I had been running the 100 metres in world record time!

Another date was fixed two weeks on from then for me to attend his surgery for a third session and I was on my way back home.

Yet again I had not been driving for long when I started to feel ill. This time it came on so fast that I threw-up over the car's passenger seat. The headaches started again and I just pulled over onto the hard shoulder and wound down the windows gasping for air.

A local police car pulled over a short time after I stopped by the side of the motorway and asked what my problem was. I showed him my warrant card and said that I must have eaten something that disagreed with me.

Happily, I started to feel better and the patrol car followed me as I drove off and tailed me until I left the motorway at Milnrow. Boy was I glad to get home safe and sound. I could not wait to go and have a lie down.

Almost right away the dreams started again and I remember tossing and turning unable to get that large bulb shaped head and black empty eyes away from in front of my face. This creature just seemed to be trying to get right inside my head. I was fighting hard and kicking out trying to throw this thing off me, but it just kept coming nearer and nearer and making that weird *minimm minimm minimm* sound.

Struggling hard to escape this nightmare I had to fight myself to wake up, which thankfully I managed to do. But I was in a cold sweat and wet all over my body. I just had to have a shower and a couple of ciggies to even start to settle myself down.

I kept wondering what these dreams could mean and if they had anything to do with the results of my hypnotic regression that was all still a total blank to me. They seemed to follow on right after each session.

I rarely have vivid dreams, at least not ones that are so powerful and memorable like these were. I understand that we all dream for some time every night but recall only a few of them, or so the 'experts' say.

Being determined to keep the after effects from the hypnotic regression a secret I decided not to tell anyone about the hell they were putting me through - especially Harry and his UFO group colleagues.

I felt that if I made too much of how ill the sessions were making me then the doctors might stop the experiment over concern for my safety.

But I knew that if that happened then none of us might ever learn the truth.

And I needed to discover that truth more than ever.

CHAPTER SIX

From Russia With Love

A couple of days had passed since my second hypnosis session and I was back on duty in Todmorden again. I never seemed to return to my village beat at Walsden now and I was sure that the vindictive inspector was manipulating the rota so that I always had to work in town so that he could watch me more closely.

I had chosen not to voice my feelings to anyone about this matter because in the force you quickly learn that if someone thinks they have got one over you and making use of that edge is causing you stress then they will just continue. But if you appear immune to their tactics they may start to look elsewhere for their wicked pleasure. So I just got on with things and pretended that I was not bothered.

On this particular morning I was going through my 'intray' in the parade room when I came across an unopened letter with a foreign looking post mark and stamps on the front indicating that it had been sent from another land.

I looked closely at this item and I could see what appeared to be a Russian postal address. I went over to one of the desks in the room and sat down - gently lifting the envelope to see if I could tell what was inside. Silly, I know, but this was quite a puzzle as I knew nobody in that part of the world and, of course, the Cold War still raged with what still remained the Soviet Union in September 1981.

Rather gingerly I opened the envelope and took out a lengthy sheaf of typed pages. The first one had an official stamp in the centre at the top and to the right hand side carried the name and address of the sender.

He was Professor Valarie Sakharov of the Institute of Science and Technology, Moscow. At first I thought it was from a woman professor but on reading the long introduction and discovering what this department was about, I soon realised that in Russia this was a man's name and that his institute were researching 'Ariel Phenomena' - or as I better knew them UFO's.

It was a very polite request expressing interest in my 'sighting' and asking if I would recount the details for him so that his department could add it to their files. The letter also mentioned another sighting where he was pursuing information and asked me about this case involving a UFO seen over Suffolk just four weeks after my encounter.

I knew nothing about any big case in Suffolk the month after mine but Jenny Randles later told me about it because she had been involved in researching that one too. Indeed at the time of this request from Russia it was not known even to most UFO researchers in the UK and the only account in print was a brief note written by Jenny in UFO publication *Flying Saucer Review,* where she had just published that introductory investigation notice about my case. Sakharov could only have read about both cases in there.

Jenny told me what she knew about these Suffolk events. A radar officer at an RAF base in Norfolk had been put in touch with her in late January 1981 after the USAF at Bentwaters in Suffolk had requested them to check for any radar tracking of a UFO. The base claimed that an object was being pursued through woods by a military patrol out of sister base RAF Woodbridge. That team was tramping through Rendlesham Forest late on 28 December 1980 – exactly a month after my sighting.

Those radar tapes were quickly assessed by the UK government which was how Jenny's contact learned that senior staff on the air base (leased by the USAF from the RAF and housing then secret nuclear arms) had seen light beams emerging as the UFO hovered amidst trees.

The airmen in the forest had recorded some of the events 'live' on audio tape and had felt strange electrical energy that made their skins tingle and hair stand on end in close proximity. One of the USAF men reportedly got close enough to touch the glass surface like UFO, but time anomalies then occurred creating disorientation. Again much of this was very familiar territory to me.

Jenny's colleague at the Manchester group – Roy Sandbach - created an oil painting seen on the next page based on what these airmen saw. It depicts the scene in the forest which – just like in my case – soon gathered sceptics who believed that they could explain what was seen..

The theory says the airmen mistook the Orford Ness lighthouse beam several miles away. You can see some similarity but these witnesses say they saw *both* things.

Slightly elevated radiation levels were reported in the ground and damaged trees found above where the UFO hovered. Two UFO researchers, Brenda Butler and Dot Street, heard from local airmen so spent years pursuing this remarkable case with help from Jenny, and together the three women published the first book to tell the story of this case in 1984 called *Sky Crash*. There have since been more UFO books written about this famous event than any other sighting apart from the much debated 'crash' at Roswell, New Mexico in 1947.

But three years before Jenny's book appeared the story of this case had only been mentioned publicly and very briefly in an interview with her by the London Evening Standard - shortly before my letter from Russia.

So why was a scientist in Moscow asking me about this largely unheard of case? And how did he know before anyone outside of a few UFO researchers that it was potentially of such significance and in some respects akin to my own?

Unaware of these questions when I first got that letter I did not see any harm in replying to the Russian professor and telling him about my encounter. I also honestly informed him that I knew nothing about the Suffolk sighting but if I did hear anything I would write again. I thanked him for his letter and that was it.

Of course, when Jenny Randles told me about the nature of the alleged events in Rendlesham Forest and its secrecy then the interest of a professor from the Soviet Union took on a different air – even though I had had no reason to suspect sinister motives behind his request.

I showed this intriguing letter to one or two of my colleagues just to prove that someone as important as a foreign scientist was becoming interested in my sighting. I viewed it as a degree of vindication after going public. I was not really thinking there could be a darker motive.

At the next local UFO meeting I even passed the letter round for the group to read and they were equally interested. Indeed I think it gave us all a boost by encouraging us that a science institute was trying to get to the bottom of whatever it was that we were seeing – all be it one behind the Iron Curtain!

It was on that night that I suggested we invite Harry Harris to give us a talk on his collection of video interviews with UFO witnesses. I think at that time we were meeting in an upstairs room at the Golden Lion Pub on Rochdale Road. I phoned Harry when I got home and told him of the invitation from the group. Harry was delighted but when I mentioned the letter from Russia he became highly intrigued and told me not to lose it or give it away to anyone.

Whilst I was speaking to Harry on the phone there was a bit of a weird echo in the background. I mentioned that I was hearing this to him but he said he could not pick up anything at his end. After we had exchanged our good byes Harry put the phone down but I waited a few seconds and then heard a small but distinct clicking noise as though someone else had just 'hung up'.

Arriving at work the following day on the 6pm to 2am shift, I went to my intray in the parade room and was relieved that the letter from the professor was still there. After hearing those noises on my phone line I had started to think up all sorts of daft things during the night and I had been unable to sleep. Indeed I was starting to become slightly paranoid about it all now. So I was very glad to find that the letter had not been 'appropriated' and just told myself not to be so silly. The noise was probably just an ordinary crackle on my phone line.

During the late evening whilst I was having a brew and a cigarette in the mess room my unhelpful 'Inspector' arrived and started a conversation with me about UFO's in general. I told him that there must be something out there and that we cannot be the only planet in the universe that has life. He agreed with me for once, which I found curious. Then he carried on for a while as though we were the best of mates, which seemed even more peculiar.

Eventually he asked me about the letter from the professor, claiming that one of the lads on the shift had mentioned it to him in passing and he wondered if it was still on the premises? If so then he would like to read it. I fibbed that it was at home but if I could remember then I would bring it in for him to have a look. I was not sure it was the right thing to say but I was by now suspicious.

In reality I was totally caught on the hop by this shock request and muttered to myself : '*No way will you be reading this.*'

Harry and Mike Sacks turned up at our house a couple of days later, as they wanted to see the letter too and over a nice cup of tea and a cigarette they examined it carefully.

Mike was particularly excited with the idea of a Russian professor being interested in UFO's given his own encounter five miles from me inside a Bacup quarry and Jenny's subsequent discovery of the involvement of possible USAF fighter planes chasing after whatever he and others had seen that night.

Harry asked if he could take the letter away with him as he wanted to contact the professor directly and I was okay with that. I also brought up the noise on the phone with them both and asked them if they thought I was getting carried away. I told them that it was happening each time I used the phone now and I was beginning to think that my line might be 'tapped'. Frankly they looked like they thought it was me who was tapped - not the phone - and Harry even asked " *Why would anybody want to do that to you?* "

I had no answer to give to such a perfectly sensible question. So the subject was closed and then they left and the letter went with them.

It was now Sunday 20 September 1981 and my third regression was set to take place - this being the second one at Professor Blair's house in North Manchester. For obvious reasons I was not looking forward to it one bit. I was having dark thoughts about how I would end up being sick once again and that those 'nightmares' would start up as soon as I got home.

Yet at the same time I did not want to let anyone down. So I arrived at the home of the doctor and we all trooped upstairs, Harry this time being allowed to set up his camera as Dr Blair was now happy to consent after discovering the nature of my case. But he still insisted that Harry, Mike and Norman all left the room whilst the Professor started the process to induce hypnosis.

After the session concluded – again seemingly in less time than it really did - I decided not to hang around and just wanted to get back home before I started to feel too sick to drive. I think I was probably rather abrupt with the three of them on departure given that I just left them sitting there full of questions and shot off. But I was not ready to tell anybody about the sickness or the weird dreams in the wake of my past sessions and so just said a hasty goodbye and left. Happily I did manage to get home this time without being physically ill but the headaches started as soon as I stepped into my car.

It was late evening by the time I arrived home and after having a shower I went straight to bed dreading what dreams might come. I woke up after a couple of hours with hot sweats across my body and knew that the weird images were back in their full horror. So I got up and had another shower and went downstairs for a cigarette and decided to have a few stiff 'drinks' to relax me. I must have emptied half a bottle of whiskey before going back to bed.

It worked – though – as I went out like a light.

In the morning I was back on duty and feeling far from my best when Malcolm Agley came into the station and related one of his infamous on the job yarns concerning a sudden death that had occurred on a bowling green during a cup final. Despite the morbid nature of the events his black humour was always funny and I started to feel better for my chuckling.

It would be unfair if I just left you wondering what this incident was about, so here is the gist of Malcolm's tale. That late Indian summer weather was hot and sunny when we had got a call to attend a local bowling club about a death. On the copper's arrival they were met by a doctor, the captain and club chairman who informed them that the deceased had collapsed on the green whilst playing in the finals and the doctor - who had also been playing - pronounced him dead at the scene.

They asked to see the body but were directed into the club house, not outside onto the green. On seeing the officer's surprise at this having expected the body to be in situ where he had died the bowlers told Malcolm and his colleague '*oh, we took him o'er there to allow play to continue reet to the end*'!

There was nothing suspicious about the death and the doctor felt that no harm was being done here. So the local undertaker - who worked for the coroner - was asked to pick up the body but he turned up in a tiny little car and informed the lads that his hearse had got stuck in the garage because some motorist had parked right across the entrance to it and blocked him in!

Not to be perturbed our lads decided to improvise and take the deceased to the mortuary in the back of their patrol car. The dearly departed was thus placed sitting up on the back seat with one of the lads located next to him for company on his final journey. Passers-by will have seen the poor chap apparently 'under arrest' though most certainly *not* in any state to help with our enquiries.

To some people it may seem strange that you can make a funny story out of grief, but a policeman must deal with stressful situations and sometimes to cope you have to detach your emotions or you will crack up.

Harry phoned me at home later on that Monday having now shown my Russian letter to Norman Collinson. The fraud squad DCI had been very intrigued by it. Harry also said he was going to write to Sakharov and introduce himself as a UFO investigator involved in both my case and various others. In fact he seemed quite excited about the possibilities of establishing international contact.

After Harry put the phone down I waited a couple of seconds in anticipation and – sure enough – heard the 'click' again. By now I was almost certain that this was real and someone was listening in to my conversations.

It would not be long before I would discover the truth. On returning to the station the following day for a shift from 2pm to 10pm I was going through my post and there was another letter from Russia. Just as I was opening it to read the shift Inspector came into the room and asked me to meet him in his office after everyone had gone out on their patrols.

Now the parade room at Todmorden Police Station is to the far left of the main front public entrance. There is another door at the front but this is for police only and must be accessed with a pin coded lock. All of this means that the officer manning the enquiry desk would not necessarily see any unexpected police operative entering the station via the other door.

So when everyone had left the station and gone out on their patrols, there was just the front desk officer and myself who remained in the parade room. I had now read the new letter from Sakharov - which was basically just a 'Thank-you' for my reply to him. The Russian institute scientist then went on to ask me once again if I had any knowledge of the UFO sighting made over Suffolk soon after my own and it mentioned the main base called Bentwaters (leased to the Americans by the RAF).

It was still a week or so before Jenny Randles would tell me more about this case when we met up at Harry's house in Sale to plan the next stages in my own investigation. So I could not yet help the Russian professor. But I was starting to feel a bit uneasy about his suspiciously high level of interest in this matter.

Just as I was pondering his request the Inspector entered the room and made hand gestures for me to follow him into his office via the back stairs and head away from the main part of the building. Another man was sat in there - I presumed a CID officer as he wore civilian clothing not a uniform.

I stood there for a few seconds before the Inspector told me to sit down and he had just started to introduce this gentleman when the man swiftly interrupted and said:- "*Just call me the man from the Ministry.*"

I stared at him. He was wearing a very thin smile - half looking down at the floor and with his first fingers from both hands tapping slowly but gently against his lips. It was a little unnerving.

"*I have been reading your report about the incident that occurred back in November of, um, last year with what, shall we call it, an* ***unusual****, if not* ***unbelievable,*** *object that you have claimed to have seen* ***hovering*** *above and completely blocking the road*" - this stranger stressed those words in a rather peculiar manner.

The man spoke in a slow and quiet voice and his odd manner of speech clashed with how he seemed to be rather well educated. He was holding a brown file cover which lay open across his knee with some papers inside that he kept glancing down at in order to read. I presumed them to be pages from my official police report on the sighting – which, of course, I had not seen.

"*Are we supposed to believe this*?" he said tapping his finger repeatedly on the file.

He then made a strange grunt - "*urumph*" - a noise that made you want to slap the face that uttered it.

I stared back at this 'Ministry' man with an expression he was not going to forget in a hurry. One of those very slow up and down looks that you give to someone that implies dismissal from consideration.

" *I couldn't care a monkeys toss what you – or even **if** you - believe it or not*" I replied to this officious gentleman. "*But that is exactly what I saw and **that*** (now pointing firmly at his file) *is exactly what did happen on that night – OK*?"

I noticed that I had emphasized words like him and raised my voice in irritation at the end. The Inspector asked me to sit down and not get so aggravated.

` "*Who exactly are you anyway*?" I asked the stranger. "*And what is all this 'Call me the man from the ministry' guff*?"

" *Patience, that's all I ask..*" he said in response - looking directly at me. "*Let me explain...*" he continued.

Then he talked about the letters that I had received from the Russian professor.

This mystery man informed me that he had read copies of both letters after they were passed onto him at his ministry office. And although there was nothing in them that would be of any real use to Whitehall they were aware of the author and his motives and – the stranger now seemed to take particular pleasure in adding... "*These motives are **not** - shall we say - what they **seem** to be.*"

As he spoke the hint of mystery behind his voice was obvious and rather chilling. It made me shiver.

The man informed me that he was aware of the

UFO incident around the RAF base in Suffolk and that my sighting was being investigated by the MOD as was that US Air Force witnessed incident but he could not go into this matter further until such time as their investigations were complete. He added that it would probably take some time as hundreds of sightings are reported every year to the Whitehall 'department'.

Next the '*man from the ministry*' asked if I had shown the letter to anyone else and I told him about Harry Harris and Mike Sacks and added the name of DCI Collinson - as having read the first letter.

He scribbled these names down onto his file then suddenly got up and left the room.

I looked at the Inspector in bemusement but before I could say anything the door re-opened and my inquisitor popped his head back in again and whispered:

"*I will be in touch*". Then he nodded and left.

As I let this extraordinary sequence of events sink in the inspector opened a brown envelope and took out a "*Minute Sheet*" - a written report sent inter department between police officers. He passed it across the desk and asked me to read it and then sign it at the bottom to confirm my acceptance.

I scanned it carefully and discovered that it was an order covering the *official secrets act*. I had signed this act when joining the force as many public servants do but this new edict forbade me from communicating with media such as newspapers, tv or radio or to discuss events with anybody outside of the force. Quite frankly the long list of things I was being reminded I must reaffirm agreement never to do was extensive in legal jargon I knew only too well.

But – I noticed, with grim fascination – the order not only covered my own UFO sighting but the events surrounding the death of Zigmund Adamski a few months earlier. Of course I signed the sheet, given my adherence to the official secrets act being necessary for being able to continue as a serving officer, but I suspect it was done this way more to put the frighteners on me. There was no obvious reason to connect UFOs with the Adamski case or why it would be subject to this sort of order. But if it was a scare tactic then it was effective.

Shortly afterwards Jenny Randles explained her then still early but escalating research into the Bentwaters case I was shocked to discover that she and her two colleagues had experienced similar problems involving phones and that these had made them suspect that they were being 'listened to' just as I had now done.

Jenny reveals: '*This did not occur regularly when I was a UFO investigator. But when Brenda, Dot and I were chasing this still 'secret' case we did experience odd clicks on the phone as we talked over details - something we had to do as I lived over 200 miles from where the others were located near that air base. We also got the run around whilst talking to the Suffolk police trying to interview an officer who we learned was called out by the USAF to view the 'landing site'. They even bizarrely told us we would be in trouble if we were recording the phone call – something we were not doing. These odd things became so persistent and unusual that we felt the sensitive nature of this encounter must have triggered some kind of interest from the government*'.

"We knew that the Ministry of Defence was investigating the case from very early on – before it was public knowledge even locally",' Jenny added. *"In fact – when Brenda and Dot first visited USAF Bentwaters six weeks after the sighting to ask questions of the Squadron Leader who was the UK liaison between the USAF and MoD they were mistakenly thought to be from Whitehall officially investigating that secret report. This had been sent to London by this RAF officer on behalf of the witnesses but was not released for another 2 years by the USAF after a Freedom of Information suit was filed in the USA. When the RAF officer realized that Brenda and Dot were civilian UFO researchers who somehow knew about a case which the USAF and MoD thought was still top secret he stopped talking and ordered them out. The man they saw that day later filed with the MoD a report of my personal theories about the Suffolk case."*

Given Jenny's revelations there was a conceivable reason why someone might want and be able to keep tabs on what investigators knew about a case that stayed out of the national media until October 1983 when it was the front page lead in the press and on major TV shows.

Indeed Jenny tells me that 30 years after our conversation the long secret records of the Ministry were released about this Bentwaters case. They revealed that a defence intelligence unit did follow it up – just as I was told. And how the MoD assessed the likely response of the UFO community to things that Jenny had raised about the case. She had discussed the possibility that the Rendlesham event might involve a mishap involving one of those secret nuclear weapons.

Jenny does not now believe that such an accident occurred, but the fact that the MoD had files noting her opinions on that possibility and contemplating how the UFO community might react to her views supports the prospect that these things were at least being monitored.

She tells me: *'It is worth remembering that at this time the women's peace movement protesting against cruise missiles at US bases in the UK was causing real trouble for the government and that protest was covertly observed. So three women jointly investigating a UFO case involving a USAF base might have looked rather suspicious in that context. And your letter from Russia about it may have attracted interest too.'*

So my 'paranoia' during that autumn of 1981 had company. Jenny adds that in 1983 - after the Bentwaters case went public - she and her fellow investigators from East Anglia, took part in a press briefing on it set up by Harry Harris with DCI Norman Collinson at a hotel in Altrincham, Cheshire. It was the last time that she saw Norman as he left the Manchester group soon after but that day he quietly showed her a 'note' that was not made public but implied that a senior figure in the Greater Manchester Force was not only aware of, but seemingly being updated about, UFO activity in major cases from 'sources' acting inside of UFO groups.

A few days after my meeting with this worrying visitor claiming to be from the MoD I spoke to PC Malcolm Agley and he informed me that he had not had himself an audience with the 'Man from the Ministry' and not been asked to sign anything new or specific over the Adamski affair either.

I kept wondering if I should talk this all over with

Harry or Mike but could see that these were dangerous waters to be treading and very likely I would only put them at risk and jeopardize my future in the police.

Soon my concerns became irrelevant when Harry phoned and said that he had just received a visit from a man working with his local police CID unit. This officer took away the letter I had loaned Harry and warned the investigator against any contact with this Russian professor.

Harry phoned me a couple of days later and told me that given these events he planned to now play the video tapes of the hypnosis sessions at his house in Sale, south of Manchester. But he warned me to be prepared to see some astonishing footage of myself reliving what he believed to be a real and true event and the 'very shocking' things that had happened that night.

With that bombshell firmly planted into my brain I was, to say the least, a bit concerned as to what my reaction would be on seeing this footage. But surely there would be some sort of logical explanation. Happily the wait was only a few days but I had to get on with life back at the 'nick' in the meantime.

Unfortunately, this took a serious turn for the worse - the sort of thing that happens and makes you wonder how you ever managed to cope with it all.

In police work there is nothing worse, especially if you are a parent, than having to deal with a tragic case involving a young child of very similar age to your own flesh and blood. Sadly, you never know when such a nightmare might be around the corner as a copper.

Beyond doubt the worst of all is the death of a child. A young life gone in a flash with the memories etched into your head forever.

One such incident happened to me as I was waiting to see the hypnosis videos. It had started out as a very ordinary day. I was driving around in the patrol car when I received a radio message to attend to an incident involving some children. They had been playing out and one of them had been seriously injured. The ambulance had already been called before I reached the spot but had not yet arrived. Without going into graphic detail all I can say is that the little lad died at the scene soon after this shocking accident.

Looking down on that little boy lying there in the road brought tears to my eyes. Then it hits you that now you must go tell the parents what has just happened. This is by far the most harrowing thing any police officer has to do. Nobody can be trained for it, there are no set of rules or instructions on how it should be done. It is just down to you and you alone.

So with a large intake of breath off I went slowly to their house and knocked on the door and as it opened I had no idea what words would come out of my mouth. I just hoped they could somehow prove of comfort.

After being invited in I took my cap off and closed the door behind me and tried my best. Once more it was the bravery of the parents that I admired that day. To lose such a precious thing as your child in any circumstances must be hard, but when it happens like this without warning it takes a lot of courage and inner strength.

This memory of that poor lad lying there lifeless in my hands haunts me years later, but the memory of how those parents coped so stoically will never be forgotten.

After such a traumatic day it was a relief when the evening saw me drive over to Harry's house in Sale and discover what I had been saying in those hypnosis sessions. I had no idea what to expect. Harry kept telling me to be prepared as though I would be watching a rerun of the apocalypse. But I knew from what little I had picked up from conversations that my account was going to be graphic and it was going to be eye opening.

Harry had promised there would be just him and Susan, his wife, present for this viewing. I settled down on the couch as Harry set up the video . Susan made us all a cup of tea and then suddenly there I was on screen.

I sat there in total silence watching myself on television, as this was the first time that I had appeared on 'the box' since in those days of just three TV channels – not hundreds - this was not something that most people got any chance to experience.

All in all it was a very strange feeling. I could not get over hearing my voice coming back at me – thinking – '*oh dear, do I really sound like that?* - it was very much a *proper* northern drawl!

But as the tape rolled on I realized that I was only relating the story as I had remembered it before and already described to many people. There was nothing out of the ordinary and I was wondering what all the fuss was about.

I was telling what I could see: *'It's a bus'* (my first thought being it was the early morning works bus, before realizing it had passed me in the town) *'No, it's not a bus. It's spinning....the top isn't spinning....there's a light on top...like a dome....I'm not going any nearer!'*

The fear in that last sentence was obvious on the tape and took me back to the memory of that moment of proximity to the UFO.

Then - in an instant - it all changed. I was getting *out* of the patrol car:- 'But I didn't ever do that!' I said to myself with a sharp intake of breath.

Next moment I was rushing back into the car desperate to escape from the object:- '*There's a bright light coming from it.. I'm off !!'* I was shouting on TV.

When had any of *that* happened? I muttered

My first filmed session was interrupted at this point because Dr Jaffe was concerned by my very obvious rising tension and said he would not continue until I was hooked up to a heart monitor for my own protection.

On screen for me sat gawping it was like watching a horror movie unfold and there was a scary panic in my voice and a very puzzled expression on my face. This was all so weird having no idea what was happening or why I had no memory of any of the things I was 'describing' until seeing this footage long after.

Suddenly the picture of me showed my mouth wide open emitting a loud *woosh* noise as I threw my arms over my eyes to shield them.

I started shouting *'Jesus the light...the light'*. It was as though I had been blinded by something.

This was the moment when the beam lit up – a part at least I had always recalled. But it was becoming increasingly weird because I remembered seeing that bright light but none of the part before it where I was getting out of the car. So these mixed sequences of what was happening were confused and made no sense to me.

By now I was sat upright on the couch trying to listen more closely because the sound on screen was limited by the inbuilt camera microphone and I did not want to miss anything I was saying.

I kept glancing over to Harry and Susan and making gestures with my hands to indicate that I had no idea what was going on or why there was a picture of me up there on screen saying these crazy things.

The video tape rolled on and I was being asked all sorts of questions by the psychiatrist and I was looking puzzled and answering him as though I was actually there on Burnley Road using the present tense in my responses unlike when you recall a memory as the past.

This whole experience was one of the most uneasy and strangest feelings that I have ever had in my life. That person on the screen *looked* like me - yet could surely not *be* me because they were talking about things that I had no memory of ever happening . It was though I was watching an actor pretending to be me reading a script I had not read. So I just sat bewildered to the end of the tape.

'I'm getting back in the car,' I was shouting on TV *'Bloody car won't go! Fffssssssh.'* - as the light poured out from beneath the object floating there above the road and right in front of me.

To this day I cannot explain why I would say what I said on that tape. Jenny Randles told me - when we sat together to watch the remaining video recordings:

'Well, Alan, I do not know what you saw or did not see or if hypnosis brings out hidden memories or just stuff from your imagination, but one thing is for sure. As you are talking there you really believe this is happening to you, because if you are acting you deserve an Oscar.'

The later tapes show the ECG machine going crazy as my stress levels rise and Dr Jaffe fighting hard to bring my trauma back under control. But his questions went on and I was coming out with amazing answers that suggested something incredible. That I had been carried or 'floated' inside this object and met a strange looking man dressed in attire from Biblical days. With him was a group of child sized, large headed 'creatures' working alongside this bearded 'human'

The man was about six feet tall and wearing a skull cap and a long white sheet or robe. He was of slim build and seemed to be smiling all the time with thin lips.

'There's something got hold of me,' my voice on the screen was now saying. *'I'm being carried....It's black....I'm floating...*They're horrible (describing the little creatures)...*they're like a little five year old lad....*(I could see myself under hypnosis visually counting them one, two, three...)...*there's eight.'*

I was scared by these smaller 'beings' and did not add more detail about them at this stage. It took a lot of effort by the doctors to get me past what seemed to be a mental block over describing those little aliens. It turned out to be because they had been touching me and 'experimenting' with me and I wanted at all costs to stop that image from returning to my head.

During the questioning by Dr Jaffe I suddenly blurted out a name -'*Joseph*'- and was, of course, asked who this was. I explained that it was the man in the robe and – and that I 'knew him'. But when asked how I knew that – I replied – '*It just came into my head.*'

At one point I was asked what was being said to me by 'Joseph' and I replied that he was not moving his mouth but his words were appearing in my mind. I know that sounds crazy. I really thought it was crazy, too, as I sat there and watched myself saying it all. But I can only describe it as I guess a sort of telepathy.

I explained that 'Joseph' wants me to get onto a bed or couch inside the room. Dr Jaffe asked if I was going to do that and my curt reply was:

'*Not bloody likely*!'

Seconds later I added: '*He's, um....I'm getting on it. I just thought about getting on it and I got on it.....There's a light....Er....I don't understand that.*'

You can see on screen how I am battling with myself to figure out these mystifying events and at the same time clearly do not want to recall them.

'I can understand him....but I can't....he's not....' I was struggling to express with words what was going on.

Then I added:

'I am ***thinking*** *what he's saying.'*

I also said another very strange thing in the final session about those child-like beings. They appeared to be 'robots' assisting Joseph. *"They are touching my Cloth"* I blurted out suddenly - but have no idea why I would phrase a reference to my clothes like that. It is certainly not an expression that I would normally use.

There was also a large black dog in that room. Why? I have no clue - perhaps it was Joseph's 'pet'.

At another point I recalled how Joseph touched my forehead and things then suddenly all went black. And I heard a voice that I repeated at Dr Jaffe's request – in a chilling deep monotone statement.

It was saying – ***'GET- ON- TO- THE- BED'***.

Whilst lying there the little 'creatures' attached some sort of bracelet onto my right wrist and my left foot around and under the instep. Then they seemed to plug into the bracelets with their long thin fingers and I describe watching a TV monitor above my head where 'graphs' appeared on the screen and I started to get severe pains inside my head. These were so bad that I became very distressed and the doctor brought me out of the hypnosis and it took some time before I came fully around. Here, it seems, was the origin of my severe headaches after recalling this part during each session.

This was the point where we all decided that enough was enough. Things were getting medically dangerous with these escalating regressions.

I looked across the room and just shook my head. Harry stood up and said something like:

"*I think we all need a large Brandy*" and left. Susan asked kindly if I was feeling alright and I blurted:-

" *He's not called Joseph he's called Yosef*" - completely out of the blue.

These words just came into my head. A few weeks later I drew Yosef's face on a blackboard in Manchester at a meeting set up the UFO team to let me tell my story.

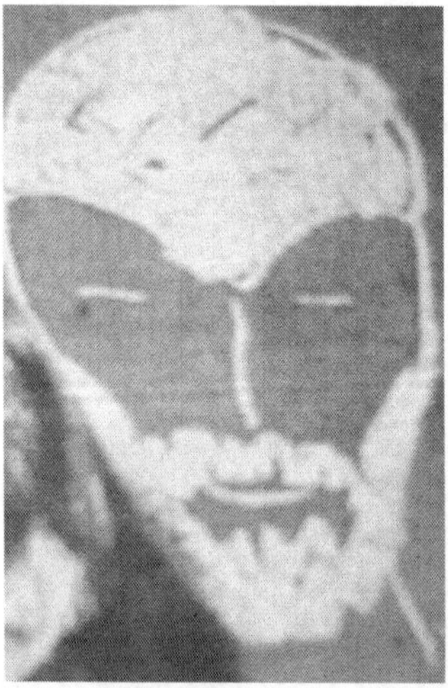

Susan and Harry are Jewish (but I had no idea as it had never come up) but I could see that the name Yosef meant something to Susan. She called Harry back into the room and asked me to repeat this latest pronunciation and both then asked me:- "*Did you know that Yosef is the Hebrew name for Joseph*?' I did not.

When I was up to watching the final video session with Jenny Randles she also asked me if I knew what Dr

Jaffe's first name was. Again I did not, but she pointed out that it was Joseph and he was also Jewish. And noted that Mike Sacks was a tailor so, of course, used to handling 'cloth'. Was this why I had used that odd term?

Whether or not some sort of 'telepathy' is any better explanation than aliens for what I came out with under hypnosis I have no idea. I just know that the way that it emerged was weird.

One thing I had noticed was how my 'story' was repeated virtually word for word in all hypnosis sessions – almost as if I was reading a script. The questions being asked by both psychiatrists in sessions held weeks apart were different but the details in my reply to them stayed unchanged. So either I was very good at remembering a 'made up' story or this was somehow a real memory.

The other thing that stood out was how during my time 'on board' this UFO something was connected by the child sized robots to my left foot. Was this 'medical procedure' the cause of that small reddish mark that had appeared on my instep immediately after my encounter and which had led me to see a doctor?

My GP had simply thought it was brought on by a sudden shock. And seeing a UFO in the early hours of the morning would qualify so I had not argued with his diagnosis. But neither Dr Williams nor myself had at that point any idea that under hypnosis I would 'relive' this probe being placed on that foot by alien machines!

Watching those video tapes was mentally draining and it was getting very late so I said my goodbyes. However, as I pulled out of Harry's driveway I noticed a dark coloured Transit van parked up the road and facing 'wrong way', which my policeman's instinct told me was not right. So as I drove past I looked back in my mirror and thought I caught a glimpse of a light inside the rear window as though someone pulled a curtain slightly open for a split second.

Or maybe I was just being paranoid again.

Even so that same van set off and followed me all the way back to Todmorden from Sale, so I pulled over and let it pass me. I took down the registration number and waited a few minutes before driving away again, only for it to reappear behind me later in my journey. I called in at the services on the motorway expecting it to follow me into there but it passed on by. Yet it reappeared once last time just after I turned off the M62 motorway at junction 21 near Milnrow.

By this point I did consider stopping and flagging it down so I could speak to the occupants but it was the early hours of the morning and quite frankly I was a bit scared as to what might happen. In the end I just drove on home but as we got to the small mini roundabout in Todmorden town centre the van turned right towards Hebden Bridge and I did not see it again.

I thought of phoning Harry the following day and telling him what had just happened but changed my mind and decided to do my own investigations so as not to get Harry involved in this mess in case my actions would bring official channels down on him. I just knew that I had to be very careful of what I did from now on. I did not know exactly who was involved or why. But either way it was probably not for my benefit.

The next time I was out on patrol in the panda car I radioed the control room at Bradford and asked for a PNC (police national computer) check - or as we would say a 10-17. Here I would give the registration number of a suspicious vehicle that I might have encountered. Well I had encountered one of those – just not right at this moment. So I gave them the number of the van that followed me on my way home from watching the hypnosis tapes.

The PNC check came back as 'No record' of any such vehicle. I then gave some mumbled excuse that I must have recorded the details wrong as normally a bogus registration plate check like this would lead to a further enquiry. Of course, I knew it was the correct number that I had written down, not a mistake, and that there was indeed something suspicious about that van.

My concerns escalated about the next regression appointment after these events. It would be the fourth one and come at the end of September 1981. Following a chat with Harry we decided it would be the final session.

Frankly, I was happy to put a stop to these grueling experiments and asked Harry if we could view all the unseen footage quickly as I needed to get this final traumatic experience over with. Jenny Randles came over to Sale to watch and put this part of the investigation to bed. She seemed stunned by how vividly I experienced the close encounter 'inside' the UFO.

But on my way driving home from that final hypnosis the usual problems occurred. I started to feel ill again and that splitting headache returned with a vengeance so I decided to pull over before I reached the motorway. Here I got out of the car and immediately threw-up, sweating and feeling dizzy.

Eventually I managed to scramble back into the car and sat there for a while and noticed in the driving mirror that another car had pulled over behind me and the occupant remained sat inside. So I kept half an eye on it until feeling well enough to set off home.

But going down the motorway the nausea returned and I pulled onto the hard shoulder where I was sick all over the passenger seat before I could get outside. I was there no more than about five minutes when I noticed a car parked some distance behind me on the same shoulder. I decided to go to the next service station to clean up myself and the inside of the car, keeping my eye on the parked vehicle which disappeared from view as I accelerated off further down the motorway.

At the fuel base of a service station I got some wipes from the kiosk to start cleaning the mess from the passenger seat. But something made me keep looking around because I still had a sense that I was being watched - call it a gut feeling. Maybe my imagination was now just running away with me but I was glad when I eventually arrived home without further incident.

After a much needed shower I retired to bed hoping for a good night's sleep but unsurprisingly was awaked shortly after I dropped off with those weird dreams.

Was I somehow reliving things that the doctors had made me remember about what happened in November 1980? Or was it nothing more than a nightmare conjured up by my own imagination and running riot after the hypnosis? After all I had read that book about the American couple who had been abducted in the 1960s and later recalled seeing aliens under hypnosis. Perhaps this had given me ideas.

I still do not know the answer to this day.

What I do know is that when the little beings were making noises that I was being asked to try to reproduce on the tape by the doctor they sounded something like '*Bi-de-bi-de-bi-de*' in a continuous drone. I was told that I had been heard making that sound in the weeks after my encounter, but before the hypnosis sessions. I was making them as noises when I seemed deep asleep.

After the regressions were over for good it was not long before I was summoned into the Inspectors office and asked to explain why I had carried on with my UFO involvement when I had been ordered not to do so.

Of course I denied that I had done such a thing and wanted to know why he thought I had, but that rebuttal gave me the first indication that my paranoia was justified. The inspector let slip that he was aware that I had been to Harry Harris's home in Sale recently and Harry was 'known' as an active part of the UFO scene. I did not deny this and, in fact, turned the tables on him and asked how he could possibly have learned that I had visited 'my *solicitor*' at his home address.

The inspector stared back but did not answer me and told me to leave his office, but I had him on the hook now and was not about to let him wriggle free.

So I asked him again but this time made deep eye contact right into his face and used an aggressive tone in my voice. He just sat there and warned me not to speak to a superior officer in such a manner.

I replied with some disgust –

"*Superior? You might be my supervisory officer but you are definitely not superior!*"

"*Get out!*" he glared at me :- "*You will be hearing a lot more about this*".

I answered with a question:

" *Well in that case, I will be wanting to know who the occupants were inside that transit van and what they were doing outside my solicitor's home. And I am sure he will be wanting a few explanations from you as well!*

"*Get out*" he said firmly but with what looked to me a hint of concern behind his eyes.

I now knew that I had badly rattled someone's cage and it would not be long before that someone would make themselves known to me.

I decided again to keep these events away from Harry as I did not think it fair to worry him about someone watching his house. After all it was looking like it was an inside job within the force. However, if someone was gunning for me and my job - then why?

Moreover, after ending the regression I was happy to go along with everything that I had been ordered to do, so this 'cloak & dagger' business was unnecessary.

I was subsequently on two mid-week days off and relaxing at home when the phone rang and I was surprised to hear the voice of the deputy head of our division on the other end. I was even more surprised when he informed me that he had been contacted by our press office at Wakefield and a journalist with the Sunday Mirror - John Sheard - who wanted to interview me regarding my UFO encounter.

Rather astonished I reminded the deputy head that I had been ordered under signature of the official secrets act not to speak to anybody, never mind the press, about my encounter or the 'Adamski' affair. I also told him about the visit from the 'Man from the Ministry' and the form I had to sign. He assured me he knew these things but it had been cleared for me to give this interview.

Nonetheless I declined and said that it was bad enough local folk knowing all about my story. I did not want it splashed across the national press. Indeed I felt very uneasy about what was going on here. This just did not sit right and I expressed my concerns to the officer and he agreed that it was my decision in the end.

But soon after I had put the phone down it rang again and this time it was the boss himself - the divisional head - a Chief Superintendent - and he started reassuring me that all would be well and that the press office would arrange everything if I agreed to cooperate.

So I said - and I do not know why I did to this day - "*Well, okay, then I will do it, but I want a supervisory officer present whilst the interview goes ahead*"

Division agreed to what I thought was a reasonable request given the form that I had been made to sign and the visit I had received from the 'ministry', but I still felt uneasy as more was going on here than I knew about. But if I had an official witness to what I was saying under request from above then I would surely have protection.

At this point I did not know that Jenny Randles had written a status report on my case for a UFO magazine so that it recorded my consciously remembered story before the hypnosis complicated things and these two sets of data could later be compared.

Nor did I yet know that John Sheard's newspaper had been trying to get Jenny to reveal my name but she had declined yet they had still written a piece about the Adamski death after talking with other sources. That story actually appeared just days after my final hypnosis session. It was misleading – suggesting that my sighting occurred on the same day that Adamski's body was found and not five months apart.

Had I read the article on Adamski first then I might have chosen not to help in a follow up. The paper said they planned to publish it on the first anniversary of my sighting – 29 November 1981.

So a short time after I had agreed with division to cooperate I received a phone call from John Sheard at the Sunday Mirror and we arranged a visit at my home address later that day. I contacted the Chief Superintendent and gave him these details and again asked him to ensure that a supervisory officer attended to give me advice and watch over things as a witness to what I then said. He assured me this would happen.

Sheard arrived a couple of hours later and we waited for quite a while but, of course, no supervisory officer ever turned up. I made a couple of phone calls asking what to do but was told that there was something 'going off' and as a result all possible officers were otherwise engaged. So I must proceed alone.

The interview itself went well but I declined to answer any questions put to me regarding the 'Adamski' affair, of course. Sheard seemed really curious over a possible 'link' between both cases. To be honest I had not thought about this. But, of course, I had been asked by my superiors not to discuss that case anyway.

During the interview a request was made for me to pose at the scene for a photo in uniform by a police car. I told him I was off duty and it would not be appropriate and in any case such a thing would never be allowed.

Silly me, a quick phone call by the reporter to division and I was in uniform together and a police car specially sent out to us and having my photograph taken on Burnley Road. This seemed really strange to me at the time and I was certainly not used to all this positive attention over my story from my superiors.

The article appeared headlined 'The Alien Terror of PC Godfrey' and was a straightforward account including mention that I had just undergone hypnosis.

Picking up the Sunday paper that was delivered to my door that morning, I could not immediately find anything and was actually relieved at thinking they had backed out – whilst at the same time a little annoyed given the time I spent.

Of course for some strange reason I had forgotten that we took the News of the World, not the Mirror, so I had to go and get one from the lad who sold the Sunday papers on the street – because unlike today - newsagents did not open on Sundays.

I can still remember the lad's face when I went to ask him for a paper. He looked at me and stared up and down and said "Front page and a double inside."

He was right and I started reading as I walked back home. My face was all over the big headline - 'PC GODFREY'S AMAZING UFO CLOSE ENCOUNTER' 'Bloody Hell!' I kept saying to myself as I walked.

My walk quickly turned into a jog. I just had to get home fast.

Shutting the door behind me I threw the paper across the hallway and sat on the stairs with my head bowed and hands clasped tightly across the crown. I sat there in total silence for several minutes when a face appeared on my lap - it's deep brown eyes staring up at me and wet nose snuggling ever closer to my groin. It was our Golden Labrador 'Brandy' - a loving old softie who must have sensed something was wrong.

I gave her a big hug and rubbed her ears as I stood up, deciding to make a brew. I was standing around waiting for the kettle to boil and Brandy was sat leaning against my legs, when I remembered that I had to go into work later that day for a 2pm-10pm shift. Worse still today of all days I would be working alongside a different set of officers on that shift.

'My god, what will they all think?' I kept asking.

"Come on girl, let's go for a walk" I told Brandy as I got the lead from behind the back door.

We went down to the park and just walked around for a bit, looking down to the floor when people passed me by. I wasn't sure what I would say if someone stopped me and started a conversation about the article. So I just kept walking and decided to go into nearby woods and let Brandy off the lead. At least there was a better chance of not bumping into someone you knew.

Back home I got ready for work and it was not as if my story would be news to anybody in the town because the local paper had run with it a year ago.

On my walk to work that black cloud that had been hanging around all morning had lifted and in fact I had a smile on my face at last, feeling ready for anything!

By chance on the way I bumped into Leonard Smith - who had seen something from the school grounds by the park on the same day as my encounter. He came over and said that there must be something going on at the police station because there were a few people gathered outside. Even a TV crew with big cameras.

"Do you think it's owt to do with the Ripper?" he suggested.

I laughed at this idea and after a few exchange of words, ignoring reference to the newspaper article, I carried on my way. Of course, I knew in my heart that camera crews at the police station would have nothing to do with the 'Yorkshire Ripper' but I was wishing it did.

Of course, as I feared they were here because of me and thanks to that article.

I decided to enter via the back door and avoid people in case they filmed me entering. fears were well founded as I had not been inside the building for more than seconds when the Inspector called me into his office. The looks I got from my colleagues were not encouraging either. I gulped in some air but this was just a taste of things to come.

Throwing the newspaper across the desk in my direction the inspector cried out: "*What the hell is all this?*"

I just looked at him, shrugged my shoulders and said nothing.

"*Right...lost your voice have you?*" He said rather snidely.

For a minute I just stood there in silence but felt this anger inside and lost my cool:

"*Who the hell do you think you are speaking to, you jumped up little prat!*"

Talk about engaging brain before opening your mouth, well this was a classic case of just that.

My inspector sat there with a mortified look in his eyes and mouth wide open. He appeared speechless. I turned and walked out, slamming the door behind me. Then - loud enough so he could hear me – I said: "*Nobody speaks to me like that.*"

I went down to the kitchen and made a brew.

"*Anybody want one*?" I shouted out but nobody answered.

So I stuck my head around the door and apart from the office man nobody was there.

"*Where is everyone?*" I enquired.

"*Out*" he replied "*And - no - I don't want a brew*".

This obviously frosty atmosphere was starting to worry me. What had I done wrong now?

I got my things together, had a quick glance at my intray and went on foot patrol via the back door. This was going to be a long shift.

I made my way to the bus station and got a lift up to Walsden where I was based that day, but straight to a friend's house. A very close friend who I knew that I could confide in without worry he would talk.

I had known Paul and Yvonne Myers for years. Paul had visited my son Darren when he was in hospital following an operation on his hip. The poor lad had contracted a disease that attacked the ball socket and made the bone structure weak and unable to carry any weight of his thigh bone. Paul had brought him all the latest video games that were around at that time and Darren loved this and proved to be a wiz with them. I never forgot that kindness.

We talked over a brew. Of course Paul and Yvonne

knew my 'story' but were shocked at the way it had been presented by the paper. I was a bit unhappy with the excitable tone, but what could you do about that? It was how they sold papers, I had grown to understand.

I swore then that I would not let another journalist near me. Some hope now the genie was out of the bottle.

Afterward I went back on the beat ready to face whatever was thrown my way, knowing that I would be in big trouble with my Inspector after our confrontation.

Unfortunately, a greater problem was building like a tidal wave. It was as yet unseen but the big one was on its way.

CHAPTER SEVEN

Things Can Only Better

I did not hear anything more from the inspector that day. Nor did I get any messages from the control room. It was as if I no longer existed so far as my bosses were concerned.

On any other day I would have been over the moon not to have yet more stressful situations to deal with. So I caught the bus back to town and made my way to the station where the night-shift was just starting to arrive. Again nobody spoke to me – in fact they just looked away as if ordered to ignore me. People who I thought were my friends behaved as if I was a stranger.

So I just got changed, left the station and made my way over to the pub. Once there I downed two pints in quick succession.

Bet and Eth - the Landlady and her sister - were good friends of mine and most of the coppers that worked at Todmorden. In fact two of Bet's own son's went on to become policemen.

"*You look like you've had a bad day Gobber*", said Bet, calling me by a nickname that she christened me with and that I still often get called by to this day.

We talked over more drinks about the article in the Sunday paper and the reaction I had received from my so called mates. Landladies must be trained to listen to their customers troubles and are a breed apart but it seemed odd that none of my colleagues had called in that day.

Still they were all due back on duty at six in the morning – on what we called a quick turn-over. They would finish one night at 10pm and be back around dawn. Thankfully I was back on my own shift pattern by then. On my way home I was wondering what reaction I was going to face when I bumped into them all again.

After drinking gallons of tea to try to get myself calm I must have gone to bed at some point because that is where I found myself when I eventually opened my eyes.

I glanced over at the clock on the bedside cabinet and it was quite late in the morning, and boy did I have one enormous headache!

Dragging myself painfully downstairs I must have had several large black coffees and a handful of aspirin to calm my pounding head – followed by a very cold shower that shook me back to life. I had the house to myself, but Brandy was once again giving me one of those looks that said she really needed a walk, which I considered not a bad idea to try to clear my head.

We went to the park where again I kept my eyes firmly locked downwards, just in case somebody passed by and decided to speak to me. Thankfully nobody did and life around me seemed to drift by quietly.

Was I being too hard on myself? Why would people be interested in my adventures anyway? The paper was probably being used for wrapping scraps by now. It was yesterday's news not a big scoop.

'Time to go to work' I said to myself as I closed the front door behind me. 'It can't be any worse than yesterday, can it?'

I mumbled these things to myself in hope but little expectation. Though as I walked into the station I was forced to reconsider:

"Here comes Captain Kirk" – was the cheery quip from what sounded like Malcolm Agley.

Indeed it was Malcolm with the biggest grin across his face as I entered the parade room. Malcolm did not realise just how much his humour meant to me on that morning. It was such a relief. But that was just like him.

The rest of the lads on shift were as friendly as I had dared hope - although the alien jokes flowed thick and fast and were pretty furious!

I felt relieved given what had happened on the previous day. So we all sat around and had a brew and I told them about the reaction from the other shift.

'*Set of wankers'* was typical of the response by the lads. They were offering me total support and I was back with my mates. It was a great feeling.

A couple of days later I got a phone call at work instructing me to attend police headquarters in Wakefield. I had to report to the 'Internal Affairs, Discipline and Complaints Department' and speak to someone there whom I will just call a senior officer. I was not looking forward to it.

I informed the lads where I was going and told them it was probably something to do with the way I had confronted that Inspector, which seemed most likely in the circumstances. They laughed when I told them what I had said in the heat of the moment:

"Trust you to say what you thought," they grinned.

It was supposed to be my day off duty but instead I faced a long drive to Wakefield. At least I had a patrol car to get me there and it only cost my free time.

On arrival I made my way down those imposing corridors and passed many administration staff - mostly policemen working as desk jockeys who looked like they needed daylight to get rid of their sallow looks.

'God just think, this lot are on the same money as the lads out on the streets - probably more given any with longer service' - I thought to myself as I waited outside the office door. Talk about front line policing.

" *Right Godfrey follow me*", said a sergeant .

" *The name is PC Godfrey to you- or Mister Godfrey,*" I responded rather hastily.

The poor officer bore a shocked look on his face. I doubt that anybody had spoken to him quite so bluntly in a while, but I think he got the message.

So I followed him through a long room with lots of desks on either side manned by yet another group of pale looking coppers, and apart from the sound of the typewriter keys incessantly clicking, they were all working in silence.

"*Sit down*" said the officer present – a chief super - when I reached him.

` "*Now exactly who gave you permission to speak to the Sunday Mirror when you had been specifically* ***ordered*** *not to speak to any members of the press?*"

He said this with a most serious look upon his face.

"*What do you mean?*" I asked in a puzzled voice. "*The police press office gave me permission. They contacted our divisional headquarters and the divisional commander* ***asked me*** *to do the interview.*'

Then added: '*So what exactly is the problem*?"

He looked shocked and a little confused by my reply as it appeared not to be what he had been led to expect. I was then asked to wait outside.

It seemed an age before I was called back in and then I was told that there had been a 'misunderstanding' and I should return to my duties back at Todmorden. No explanation or apology was offered.

I was about to leave when I suddenly remembered that it was my official rest day and I had been called in on duty so I must ask the super if he would sign my pocket book to explain why I had driven one of our patrol cars to Wakefield. This was normal practice if you had days off cancelled for police business such as attending court to give evidence at short notice.

Hence my polite request.

"*Get out!*" the officer screamed at me as if stunned by my innocent request.

I left but with a huge smile across my face. And even better, because there had been no mention at all about crossing of swords with that vengeful inspector!

For a while I hung around the large car park, having a cigarette and decided to go and have a cup of tea in the staff canteen - just off the main corridor back inside the building. As I sat there looking at all the headquarters personnel having their break, mostly dressed in nice clean uniforms with shinny shoes and ironed shirts, I could not help but think to myself:- 'Arse lickers!'

I returned to the patrol car and was about to drive back to Tod when I noticed that the chief was now standing by a car across the way with a man who seemed to have a familiar face. So I sat there unobserved by anyone, as my patrol car was one of many police vehicles parked around the building. After a while the other man shook hands with the officer and got into a car and headed for the exit, right across my path of vision.

I turned my head slowly so as not to let him see me

full on as he passed but I was sure I could identify that face. It was the so-called '*Man from the Ministry*' who had grilled me in Tod station and 'warned me off'.

What was he doing here today? - I wondered.

Wickedly I considered 'tailing' him but decided to keep distance between us as he drove towards the M1 motorway where he then took the southbound slip road and headed in the direction of London.

I took the M62 junction towards Todmorden with all sorts of questions racing through my head as to what exactly was going on. Even so I felt really happy for the first time in ages on that drive back. In fact I kept laughing out loud when I thought of the look on the senior officer's face as he was forced to back down over what he had no doubt been told by others was my deliberate act of defiance to ignore the document I had signed. He assumed I 'ran blabbing' to the national press. In fact I had been requested to do it.

Plus I was glad not to be caught up any longer in that unreal world in which those grey faced people worked. I could never bring myself to do that kind of job even if anyone were ever daft enough to ask me to do so.

I was nearly back in Tod when I heard a message come over the radio informing the Alpha Bravo 3 patrol car that there had been a serious road accident and ordering them to attend. As the location was not far from where I was about to pass I put the blue flashing lights on and made my way rapidly there figuring I might be closer than the response car and lives could be at stake.

As I approached the scene I came upon a long

tailback of traffic held up by the recent accident and in the distance could see that a very large heavy goods vehicle was strewn across the road. On even closer approach I found a small saloon car embedded under the front of the truck. It was badly crushed.

People were out of their stranded cars and some just stood around - though a few brave souls were trying to undo the car's door and get at the driver who was trapped inside the twisted metal. I told them to get back from the scene as there was a risk that the stricken vehicle might explode in flames.

Hurriedly, I ran back to my car and ordered up the emergency service equipment clearly required to effect a rescue and not long after the Alpha Bravo 3 patrol car appeared on the scene followed by an ambulance.

I had rushed back to the battered car and tried to open the driver's door but it was impossible to budge given the extent of the damage. Minutes later the Fire service arrived and set about using their 'jaws of life' gear to free the driver.

As I stood close by I could see that it was a woman who was trapped within and she appeared to be unconscious. Eventually the firemen's heavy equipment forced the door off and ambulance crew entered the vehicle and attended to her.

I could see from the look on their faces that her prognosis was grim, but they managed to get the woman into the back of their vehicle. Tragically she died soon after reaching hospital.

There is not a lot that you can say when this kind of thing strikes out of nowhere, but it seemed harder somehow that day to face such grief at close hand.

As a police officer you face a lot of accidents and you have to try to harden yourself to deal with them professionally, but this one hit home with me being on the scene yet having to watch a young life ebb away.

It was a terrible end to that day. But another huge shock was waiting when I returned to work later that week and I went through my intray. Here I found an internal minute sheet informing me that I was being transferred to Wakefield - 40 miles from Todmorden. A police house had been allocated for me there.

I was gob smacked to read this news and you can imagine my anger. This sudden transfer was impossible. With a young family it was incredibly disruptive and quite obviously being done for that very reason. In those days the police could only move you 12 miles from your home station - in my case that meant no further than Halifax - but after making enquiries with my local Federation Officer, it appeared that they could transfer me a longer distance in exceptional circumstances if they did so entirely at the force's expense. But they only ever did it if someone badly wanted you gone.

Needless to say I was very unhappy, but determined not to give up without a fight. So I went to see my best friend and colleague PC Jack Brierley, to mull things over as we would always do if either one had a bit of a problem. We sat in his kitchen for hours going over different ways to approach the sudden posting when Jack came up with a brilliant idea.

That night I replied to the minute sheet accepting the transfer but added my regret that my family could not move with me because of their commitments. My children were settled in school and we could not disrupt their education at this stage. Then - as a final postscript to the minute - I added that the Sunday Mirror was working on a possible follow up to the article about me that the force had just asked me to cooperate with. The paper considered the new twist involving a sudden transfer might form a human interest angle for a sequel.

It worked better than I ever imagined and I got a reply just a few days later without explanation but saying that the move was now cancelled!

I knew after this that I must be on my guard at all times. There were people in power who seemed desperate to mess about with my life and disrupt my role in the police in any way possible. So I had to make sure not to put a foot wrong, which was never easy in my job. But those mates on shift were keeping an eye on me too and that made a big difference.

Despite all of their best efforts I did get myself back in the sights of the big wigs at Wakefield HQ soon enough. The trouble was that when something goes on that is just not morally right I find it hard not to try to help the wronged party regardless of the consequences for myself. Such a problem came my way.

I was in charge of the front desk on our shift one evening with my personal radio switched on to what was happening in our Sub-Division. This was useful when I was stuck inside the station on paperwork as it kept me abreast of things that were happening around town and across the Calder valley in Hebden Bridge and Sowerby Bridge. You never knew would someone might need urgent assistance that I would be able to mobilise.

That night a message came over for Alpha Bravo 3 patrol car to attend a factory in Todmorden because the alarm was sounding and indicating a possible burglary in progress. This was not unusual and such calls were often false alarms, but you had to check them out, of course. Then one of the officers barked over the radio a need for immediate back-up at the factory as there were 'Men on site' - a reference to seeing people in the building who should not be there suggesting an actual burglary might be ongoing. This was now an urgent job.

I immediately informed my Inspector and Sergeant who were together in the station and they said that they would both attend. However, a good five minutes went by and they were still talking to each other without reacting to the call so I again went in and reminded them of the urgency of the request for assistance. But it was another five minutes before they left the station to go to the factory, by which point another patrol car - Alpha Bravo 5 - had arrived all the way over from Hebden Bridge and got there before them.

Sadly that other patrol car reached the crime scene just too late. The persons who had broken into the building and triggered the alarm had escaped moments before the Hebden Bridge vehicle arrived.

There was a lot of flak following this unfortunate incident, but the inspector puzzlingly delegated the official recording of our station's activity log to the most junior probationary officer involved. She had not been in the job very long and so the other copper that had been on the shout with her had to help show how to record all details of the crime. Nothing wrong with that as it was good experience to learn the job.

Sadly this would evolve into the most disgraceful act of bullying by a senior officer that I ever confronted.

We called this WPC ‘Middy Mouse’ because she was small for a copper. So I will simply refer to her as ‘Middy’ from now on. She was well liked by the other members of our shift and needed guidance in the same way as all young police officers do in their early days.

Soon after the factory incident she was put on the front desk as part of her training, whilst I was out on foot patrol in the town centre. Then I received a radio message to return to the station and take over the front desk, because ‘Middy’ had an interview with that Inspector. This was normal practice as probationers had frequent interviews whilst they progressed through their first two years of service. So I thought nothing of the matter and returned to the nick right away.

On the desk I was catching up on some paperwork whilst answering the phone and dealing with people that came in for one reason or another, such as to produce their documents after being involved in some misdemeanor. Then ‘Middy’ came down from the Inspectors office and into the control room and I could see that she was very close to tears and extremely upset. In fact she was visibly shaking.

“*Here - come on, sit down. What on Earth is the matter*?’ I asked as I helped her into a chair.

Middy showed me her report that had been submitted regarding the 'Incident' over the break in. It had been altered and sentences crossed out and then rewritten all over by the Inspector, who she told me had threatened that her job was on the line unless she agreed to rewrite it his way. She then showed me her pocket book where again her entries had been altered.

This made my blood boil as this man was trying to manipulate a young inexperienced officer into altering her report in order to show himself in a better light.

In fact it was more serious because he had altered the times of his arrival at the scene of crime making it appear that he got there earlier than I knew he had done because of the long delay after I had first informed him of the urgent need for backup. I was only too aware that had the inspector gone to the scene when I first informed that the robbers were on site that these criminals would likely have been apprehended.

Of course, that inspector knew this himself and was trying to shift attention away by using this young WPC's inexperience to get him off the hook and asking her to falsify the correct times that would reveal the truth.

I advised 'Middy' to do as ordered and rewrite her report, which she did. But then I also took possession of her original record with all of its glaring alterations. I also requested 'Middy's' pocket book with her altered original case notes – just for safe keeping.

Once finished I went into the Sergeants office and informed him that 'Middy' would require a new pocket book. Of course, he asked why and I told him - since this was not the same sergeant who had been involved in the debacle with the Inspector during the 'Incident' and was a fair man who I knew needed to hear the full facts.

The Inspector then came down from his office and asked 'Middy' if she had finished rewriting her report. She said she had done so and handed it over to him. He then asked where her original copy was and I informed him that it was now in my possession along with her pocket book.

You should have seen the look on his face. Naturally he demanded that I hand them both over, but I refused. He even threatened me with disciplinary action if I did not obey his order. So I invited him to do this but I still would not hand them over. Before he left the station I told him that if 'Middy' should face any consequences as a result of his 'interference' in her documentation of the facts then it would come back to haunt him. I would make sure of that.

'Middy' was still very upset and I brought the Sergeant out of his office to speak to her and reassure her that she was in no way at fault.

Now this Sergeant, who was nicknamed 'Big Red' on our shift, was totally different to some others. He was one of the lads and well respected by all. I knew that he would stand by his officers, no matter what got thrown in our direction and trusted him to support Middy.

I was proud and privileged to have worked with that man. He later went on to be promoted to Inspector - a well-deserved honour for someone who was honest and unafraid to do the right thing in the old fashioned way.

Big Red listened to what Middy had to say to him and I confirmed every word of her story. He did not hesitate and contacted our shift Inspector who was then off duty and at home. The officer came into the station right away and was another of the old school of policemen who stood by his squad.

He was furious when told what had happened and immediately got down to writing his own report to the Chief Constable about this sordid affair.

It was about that point when I began to grasp the serious extent of the problems that I had triggered. Instead of trying to keep my head down after the press revelations, I was bringing even more attention onto myself and making new enemies. Just what I did not need, but all unavoidable because it was the right thing to do here and I had to stand by this young policewoman.

The word soon got out and I was contacted by the control operative from our sub-divisional office at Sowerby Bridge. He had been on duty that night and recorded all the times that were relevant to the factory incident as part of his job. He was equally upset about the conduct of that Inspector as his recorded timings proved that Middy was right. So this controller was not going to lie over the facts either. He forwarded a written statement about the events along with the recorded times of officers arriving and departing from the factory. This independent evidence was damning, as Middy and I both knew that it would be.

I passed that statement on to our Inspector together with my own account and the testimony of the other PC who worked with Middy that night. All the lads were really upset about the way that she had been threatened with the loss of her job if she did not falsify this report.

I felt that this man should not be in a position of authority within the force given what he had done. Unfortunately, at his subsequent disciplinary hearing in front of the Chief Constable he was indeed found guilty but only reduced in rank to Sergeant. That at least vindicated what I had done to protect Middy, but left him still in the force as her superior officer.

Thankfully I never crossed paths with him again but 'Middy' did and in the end quit the job. I expect she just had enough of trying to do the right thing.

Weeks passed and the fuss over the Sunday Mirror story receded into the background. I had by now started to work with Jenny Randles on fully documenting my story to form a part of a book that she was writing on UFO events occurring in the Pennines.

As this was in the days before e mails and mobiles, Jenny was recording each chapter she wrote that mentioned me onto a cassette tape and sending them to me so that I could check what she was writing for accuracy in my spare time. By now she had bought a house with her fiancé and moved to Wallasey and had a job presenting regular items on Radio City in Liverpool, so making frequent trips back to Yorkshire was difficult.

Little did either of us know when we started this simple process that we were not the only ones interested in what was being written. The cassettes were taking a long time to travel back and forth as if being intercepted en route. I did wonder if someone else was keeping an eye on what Jenny was writing about me. Later I was informed that the police did indeed knew we were swapping these tapes although never how or why.

Whilst this was happening I was going through my in-tray one morning and found another letter from Professor Sakharov. By then I was much more suspicious about whether it had reached me directly or after being read first by the 'Man from the Ministry' as my tape communication with Jenny seemingly was.

Perhaps my imagination was starting to run riot, but if they knew about the tapes then surely my correspondence with Russia could not be safe?

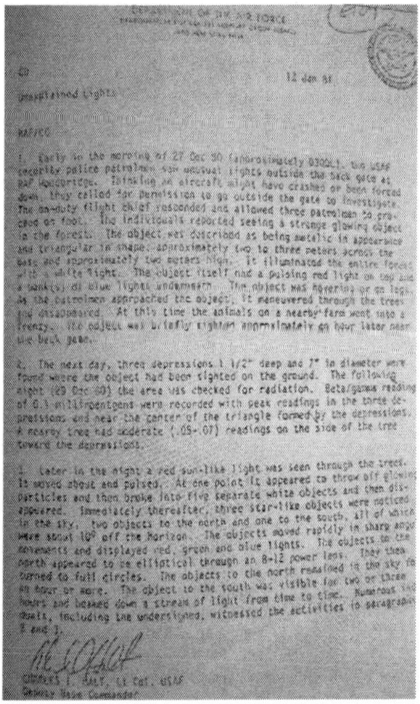

DEPARTMENT OF THE AIR FORCE

CD 13 Jan 81

Unexplained Lights

RAF/CC

1. Early in the morning of 27 Dec 80 (approximately 0300L), two USAF security police patrolmen saw unusual lights outside the back gate at RAF Woodbridge. Thinking an aircraft might have crashed or been forced down, they called for permission to go outside the gate to investigate. The on-duty flight chief responded and allowed three patrolmen to proceed on foot. The individuals reported seeing a strange glowing object in the forest. The object was described as being metalic in appearance and triangular in shape, approximately two to three meters across the base and approximately two meters high. It illuminated the entire forest with a white light. The object itself had a pulsing red light on top and a bank(s) of blue lights underneath. The object was hovering or on legs. As the patrolmen approached the object, it maneuvered through the trees and disappeared. At this time the animals on a nearby farm went into a frenzy. The object was briefly sighted approximately an hour later near the back gate.

2. The next day, three depressions 1 1/2" deep and 7" in diameter were found where the object had been sighted on the ground. The following night (29 Dec 80) the area was checked for radiation. Beta/gamma readings of 0.1 milliroentgens were recorded with peak readings in the three depressions and near the center of the triangle formed by the depressions. A nearby tree had moderate (.05-.07) readings on the side of the tree toward the depressions.

3. Later in the night a red sun-like light was seen through the trees. It moved about and pulsed. At one point it appeared to throw off glowing particles and then broke into five separate white objects and then disappeared. Immediately thereafter, three star-like objects were noticed in the sky, two objects to the north and one to the south, all of which were about 10° off the horizon. The objects moved rapidly in sharp angular movements and displayed red, green and blue lights. The objects to the north appeared to be elliptical through an 8-12 power lens. They then turned to full circles. The objects to the north remained in the sky for an hour or more. The object to the south was visible for two or three hours and beamed down a stream of light from time to time. Numerous individuals, including the undersigned, witnessed the activities in paragraphs 2 and 3.

CHARLES I. HALT, Lt Col, USAF
Deputy Base Commander

The letter again sought my help on that big UFO case in Suffolk 4 weeks after my own. I knew about those events now thanks to Jenny and in May 1983 **this** amazing report sent to the MoD by witness, USAF Col Charles Halt, went public. But only thanks to the US freedom of information act as it stayed top secret in the UK despite Jenny requesting a copy. MoD Documents later show how they dithered as she was vetted all the way up to the government minister for defence.

All of these things focused my mind on the questions outstanding from my recent visit to Wakefield. What was this 'Man from the Ministry' doing with that officer at headquarters on the very day I was called in?

My thoughts were running wild trying to grasp why someone from the MoD was even interested in matters like these. Did they really think aliens were here? Was that the reason for such cloak and dagger activity?

It was true that this department was the place to where the reports of my UFO sighting had been sent by headquarters along with any other significant sightings made by police officers whilst on duty. But why would they want to follow up mine in this way and not others?

I was beginning to have doubts about this person's proclaimed origin from Whitehall. He was acting more like a man who knew his way around the inside of the police force. At the very least he obviously had some 'clout' with my inspector and in Wakefield , implying that he had some sort of authority over senior officers.

I needed to ponder the discoveries that Jenny made about the MoD taking serious note of what UFO researchers thought during cases like that secret memo on the previous page. And the note to Norman Collinson she saw from a senior police officer implying the force got information from 'sources' inside UFO groups. Given all that it did not look quite so paranoid after all.

So I took the Sakharov letter home with me and put it in a safe place, before, after a couple of days, deciding it was best to burn it in the garden with some rubbish.

I really was starting to think dark thoughts about all of this and one thing was starting to hit home. There was an escalating campaign against me. I could only assume the reason to be that I had talked – though with police approval – about something strange that I saw whilst on duty on Burnley Road.

Why was there such a big deal about that? It was just a sighting of something in the sky and many police officers had seen things themselves and reported them without that over reaction. Norman Collinson's report from Heywood, for example. Or the officers looking for those stolen motorcycles out of Halifax. So why just me?

A week later I discovered that there had to be some reason because it clearly was a very big deal to someone out there.

I got a minute sheet at work requesting me to attend Wakefield headquarters yet again, but this time for a medical examination with the Force Surgeon – officially regarding the injuries that I had received in that attack outside the station back in 1977.

I could not believe that reason. Those horrific events had by now been over five years earlier so why did I suddenly need a medical for them?

They had not bothered about this when I was in hospital facing an uncertain future, nor paid this level of attention when consigning me to painful push bike duty even after I protested against it on medical grounds. Their concern for my health looked very one way.

This was certainly starting to look like a coordinated and escalating attempt to get rid of me at all costs and by any means they could come up with that would eventually work.

It turned out that these simmering concerns were sadly justified and there was someone really out to 'get' me.. This campaign was not merely in my head – it was very real and about to enter a frightening phase that would expose once and for all just how far these dark forces were willing to go.

I was about to face the terrifying prospect that they might stop at nothing to get their way.

CHAPTER EIGHT

A Friend In Need....Is A Friend Indeed

I had a couple of days to mull over the minute sheet and take in what might be going on. So I decided to visit my mate Jack Brierley at home rather than chat to him at work where 'walls have ears' – as they say.

After what had been happening I was taking no chances. Especially if they were now going after my health.

Although I had some good mates within the job, there were those that I did not feel able to share sensitive and important issues with like these, but Jack was someone that I knew would never repeat anything that we might discuss in private.

Big Malcolm Agley was another I could depend upon, but he lived in Hebden Bridge, so it was easier to pop over to Jack's house as he lived local. You could bounce worries off him without feeling that you were making a mountain out of a molehill.

Jack would never laugh at your concerns, but had a habit of coming up with ideas and suggestions that sometimes put a different perspective on things that you had not considered before.

That day we talked for hours and in the end both agreed that the Force Surgeon - Dr Ellis – was not the kind of man that would deliberately set out to have me discharged on medical grounds without very good reason to do so. And there was surely none to be found – given that my injuries, if not fully resolved, were at least considerably improved after several years where I had worked on in service without such concern from above. Given his reputation we felt he would not just bend under pressure from someone, no matter who that person was. He was a well-liked and respected medic amongst all the rank and file of the West Yorkshire constabulary.

I felt a lot better after talking with Jack and stopped worrying so much about the examination – until I arrived at the Wakefield headquarters and saw a familiar face heading towards me down the corridor.

You guessed it - there he was again – the 'Man from the Ministry' was on my case once more.

He was busy talking to an officer whom I thought I recognized so I slipped quickly past into an adjacent office before they spotted me on the corridor.

" *Could you tell me where the Force Surgeon is situated, please ?* " I asked one of the typists who sat nearest the door as I tried to appear sufficiently lost and bewildered in front of her.

She had to repeat the directions a couple of times, just to make sure I took it all in but, of course, I was just waiting for the coast to be clear before I ventured back into the corridor. Happily when I did so it was now empty, though I could not help wondering what this mystery man was doing here yet again on the same day as me and why he was on such good terms with what looked like the chief super from internal affairs.

Gingerly I made my way towards Doc Ellis's room, keeping a sharp eye out for those two.

On entering the surgery Dr Ellis greeted me with a warm and friendly smile, shaking hands across his desk and indicating for me to sit.

" *How are you Alan, good to see you again, it's been a long time since we last met*" he said warmly.

I nodded to acknowledge the fact. "*It must be at least four years*"

" *Ah - yes, I put you on light duties, didn't I, because of your injuries following that horrific attack?*"

This was not really what I wanted to hear, so I fired back reassuringly:

" *It was, but I really am fine now, doc. I signed myself off them soon afterwards because I got fed up of being desk bound...Now I'm as fit as a fiddle*"

The doc peered at me:

"*Mmm, really? That's not what I've been hearing,*

or reading on this file of yours... I've just had a visitor, well two of them actually. They seem to think otherwise. So what are we going to do about it ,eh?"

There was a devilish hint of a smile at the end.

I shrugged my shoulders, but did not let on that I suspected who his 'visitors' were. I am reasonably sure that they were the man from the ministry and the person who looked like the chief super from internal affairs.

Doctor Ellis nodded sagely, then looked at me with resigned but kindly eyes after considering my notes once again and then carefully inspecting my appearance:

"Well you look pretty fit to me - physically at least - and you do not appear to be suffering any kind of mental disorder from what I have seen so far. Certainly nothing that would require me to recommend that you are medically unfit to carry on with duties as a constable.'

What do you think then Alan...Am I right?" He asked softly.

He beamed a smile in my direction and it was one of those knowing expressions from someone aware, but not supportive of, what others were asking him to do to me. I knew immediately he would do right by me.

The surgeon continued:

" *I am going to sit down and write a report to the Chief Constable about what has gone on today. I shall be informing him that you are in good health - both physically and mentally."*

Then he added with a twinkle:. *"I shall also ask him to make an appointment for the person that ordered this medical for you. I want* ***them*** *to come and see me for a check up on their own health and welfare - as I am not too sure about the status of that right now."*

I just chuckled inwardly at his fully intended jibe, before he added with a more serious tone:

" *Alan, just watch your back, there are people out there who are determined to do you harm in any way that they can. To be blunt - they want you out, and will stop at nothing until they succeed."*

I thanked the doc and left that room – just happy that his short time in my presence let him see through the plot being railed against me.

However, now I was left with a lot more to ponder as it was obvious my brooding fears about a vendetta were apparent even to outsiders.

They want me out? But why?

I kept my eyes wide open, looking behind me as I moved quickly along the corridors on the way out watching for anything that might seem out of the ordinary. It felt mildly absurd doing this, of course – *just get a grip* I whispered to myself at one point – you are in the police headquarters for goodness sake. What can possibly happen to you in here?

But there was no doubt that I was really spooked after what Dr Ellis had just told me and relieved when I reached my car to drive off.

The cigarettes tasted ever so satisfying all the way back to Todmorden. But I did not go straight to the station and detoured to Jack's house instead. I knew he was off duty that day and would be at home and I needed to sit down and have a good natter with him about what had just gone on. I told him what the doc had said and he looked very puzzled and shocked.

"Better keep your head down and do now't stupid... we'll sort things out if needs be...so just hang in there pal...all will be well, you'll see".

Those were words that I needed to hear that day and I relaxed before going back on duty.

On my arrival I went into the parade room to check my in-tray and see if there was anything relevant that had been going on whilst I was away and was pleased to find nothing out of the ordinary – particularly no further letters from Russia. That was a complication I did not need right now.

At the end of my shift off came the tunic and tie, on went my jacket, and I signed off to head straight to the pub. The first couple of pints went down a treat, but Bet - the landlady - could sense that there was something up with me and did try her hardest to find out what it was. Of course, I remained quiet about what was bothering me and talked only about things in general. Luckily there were only the two of us present.

Then I heard the front door open and the door to the pool room, followed by the sound of balls being discharged from the table. Bet went to see who it was, and I heard her speak firmly to the customers in there.

"I have told you two that you're barred from here, now go".

She glanced back at me and I knew she wanted assistance, so nodded and got off the bar stool just as one of the youths brushed past her and entered the gents toilet. I could hear the other one saying that he had 'put money into the pool table so they were **going** to play'. I did not like how disrespectful they were being to Bet.

So I followed into the toilet where the other man was relieving himself. Moving behind him he shuffled against the wall and turned slightly. I could sense him wondering how to react but kept my emotions in check however badly he and his mate had treated Bet.

Keeping him pinned by my body against the urinal for a second I said: " *You heard the lady...now piss-off*'.

Having stood back to let him move he turned and for a split second I thought he was going to attack me, but he suddenly became aware of who - or rather from my uniform *what* - I was, and left the toilet whilst beckoning his mate to follow him rapidly out of the pub.

I needed a stiff drink after that and Bet duly obliged with a wee dram of whisky. Needless to say it was dark by the time that I got home and I was a little bit on the tiddly side of sober.

I did not know it then, but this was just the start. This routine of me going for a drink after work to calm my nerves because of a constant need to guard against forces plotting behind my back had turned into a habit. It was not just after the evening shift. I was doing the same after the afternoon shift and things were starting to get out of control. Yet sadly like most heavy drinkers I thought I could handle it.

Of course, I was wrong.

A few days later I was in plain clothes getting ready to leave the house to do some observation in Centre Vale Park on the look-out for a 'flasher' that had been exposing himself to schoolgirls on their way to the high school. I was just about to leave when Jack pulled up outside in a patrol car and informed me that I had to go to Wakefield for yet another medical, but this time to the Stanley Royd Hospital in town. He had been ordered to drive me there right now with no warning.

We had a brew and discussed the situation, and decided that this sudden act was deliberate. Jack agreed to accompany me into the consulting room when we arrived. It was a long drive and I was getting very nervous about the whole thing so needed his support.

"*Jack - you stick to me like a blanket and don't leave me on my own!*" I said as we neared Wakefield.

As we approached the building I asked Jack to pull over and I got out of the car and told him I would not be a minute. I had just had a brave – maybe totally foolish – brainwave when we passed a shop. But I was now in full self-preservation mode worrying about what my enemies had up their sleeves in their latest act of desperation.

I rushed across the road to a 'Dixons' Electrical store that was on the high street and came out with a big grin on my face.

"What have you got there Gobber ?" asked Jack, spying the bundle in my hands.

"A bit of security you might say" I told him mysteriously.

We both looked at each other and started to laugh as he saw what I held.

"You are surely not being serious! You ***can't*** possibly *do that!"* Jack grinned as he realized my intentions.

" *Just watch me...two can play at this devious game*" I told him in a determined voice – and off we went.

Arriving at the hospital and driving into the grounds we both looked at each other and neither said anything for a moment as we took time to digest my suicidal plan.

We just looked around at the old Victorian buildings which reminded me of some long gone work house or sanatorium where people written off as 'lunatics' were once locked away for life with no hope of getting the help and care that they really needed.

It sent a cold shiver down my spine.

"This place doesn't look good...rather you than me" Jack said with one of his mischievous expressions.

"Don't be such a prat and remember ***never*** *leave me on my own for God's sake!"* I told him, before adding: *"Now let's find a toilet so I can prepare myself*

and get set up before they send for me!"

We drove around the grounds until we found a parking space and then walked along the paths that ran between the manicured lawns and flowerbeds towards the entrance. The nerves were getting to me now and I had this sickly feeling in my stomach.

Jack kept reassuring me that everything would be alright but it was not him about to be 'examined'. And I was the one preparing to enact a scene from *Mission Impossible* that could save my future or terminate it.

Once inside, that smell of hospital hit me smack in the face and made me feel even worse. I briefly turned to walk back outside unsure if I could proceed, but Jack stopped me in my tracks and gave me one of his looks .

'*Get a grip'* , he chided - then glanced his head in the direction of some toilets near to the entrance:

"Come on...get in there and sort yourself out."

I went inside one of the cubicles and began to assemble my 'secret weapon' - a mini tape-recorder that I had just purchased at the store together with a tiny microphone that you could attach and hide out of sight.

After I had inserted the batteries I switched it on and went back into the washroom and recorded my name rank and number, plus time, date and place and Jack obliged by speaking his own identity for moral support. We rewound the tape and played the recording. It had worked a treat and picked up everything that was said.

The recording time on these micro cassettes back then was 60 minutes each side. With one of them loaded I was ready for anything and could face what the police were about to throw at me.

I knew that I was taking a risk with this secret taping but given what was going on behind my back and recalling those words from Doctor Ellis it was a gamble I felt I must take for my own protection.

We left the toilets after re-recording our introductions again – for purposes of evidence this time - and made our way to reception where I was 'booked-in' and told to wait in a small room off the corridor.

It was not long before a 'Nurse' came into the room and spoke to Jack, who was in uniform whilst I was not because of my flasher patrol duty requiring plain clothes She asked him if I was 'Alan' in a rather condescending voice. So it was with a slightly annoyed tone that I asked her if she should speak to me directly, please.

"I'm not deaf, you know, I can speak for myself."

She looked shocked at my bluntness but I had enough of being treated like a nutcase when I had done nothing to deserve that and she quickly got the message.

After what seemed like ages she came back into the room and asked Jack to follow her and bring me along. I think the look we both gave to her then was enough and she quickly apologised with a smile.

"It's the uniform, ' She said regretfully.

'I am thinking that he looks like your police escort

...I'm so sorry."

As she turned to go I switched on the recorder and gave Jack a little wink and a tapped my forehead to indicate that I was more determined than ever to have hard evidence of what was about to take place.

Jack followed me into the room where there was a long desk with two smartly dressed gentlemen seated side by side and facing the door. In the corner, to the right of them both, was a lady who was seated back against the wall with a notebook on her lap and a pen in her hand.

There was only one seat available to the front of the desk where one of the gentlemen made a hand gesture for me to sit. I stood there for second or two and asked that another be made available for Jack and they looked surprised – making clear that they were opposed to having anyone else 'sit in' during my 'consultation'. I informed the doctors that if Jack left then so would I….and they grudgingly agreed to my request.

Jack sat at the back of the room just behind me but to my left, so if I turned my head slightly I could see him out of the corner of my eye. Just the fact that I could do this that meant I knew I was not alone and allowed me to relax in these increasingly surreal surroundings.

The two gentlemen introduced themselves by name and informed me that they were both consultant psychiatrists and were requested by the West Yorkshire Chief Constable to determine my state of *mental* health.

After confirming that I understood this the

inquisition started in earnest and neither man pulled his punches. It seemed to go on for hours but Jack was keeping his eye on the time because when one hour was nearly up and the tape set to finish, we had planned that he would make an excuse to go to the loo and we would both go together, allowing me to turn the tape over.

The questions from these psychiatrists were relentless and I found them demeaning. At times they seemed to be very personal about my childhood and asking how my parents had treated me. They quizzed about my sexuality and many more things that were difficult to find relevant to what had happened over Burnley Road and nothing at all to do with the injuries inflicted on me years before.

Then they started to ask me questions about the 'hallucinations' that I had been suffering from. Straight out with it - there was no pussyfooting around. As far as they were concerned that was what I had been accused of experiencing. The object over the road was in my mind – when there was so much evidence it was real like the marks on the road seen by others.

Well at this point I hit the roof and demanded to know what they were talking about. They advised me of a report sent to them by a senior officer - or to be accurate, as actual names were not used - 'from Headquarters'. Based on the content of this report they had been asked to ascertain my general state of mental sanity and what treatment would be required to ensure that I was able to carry on working for the police, or whether I should instead be discharged as 'unstable'.

I was dumbstruck at this turn of events, but Jack intervened in my defence and demanded to know where such loaded questions were heading. He also told them that I was by no means the only policeman who had ever seen a UFO in and around Todmorden and added that plenty of others had witnessed such things, plus many upstanding members of the public.

So were all of these people suffering from hallucinations too?

I reminded that I had worked normal duties on the day before and was rostered on duty when driven here by Jack and had full service since my sighting a year ago - so what had suddenly led to this investigation?

They looked shocked by Jacks intervention and the facts that I just stated. They appeared to assume that I had been signed off on the 'sick' after being accused of 'seeing things'.

Then Jack came out with a cracker that still brings a smile to my face:

" *When you are going home tonight and you come across a strange craft or some lights in the sky and it comes down and blocks the road in front of you, what will you chaps do?'*

He let that question sink in for a moment then continued:- *'Well I tell you what you will do - one of two things - pretend that you never saw it and say nothing to anyone...or you will call the Police and make a report....well Alan was that policeman who did his duty...get my drift? It would not matter what you personally believe about these things, if it happens to you then that is all that counts.* ***You tell the truth.*** "

At that we both stood up to leave but were stopped in our tracks when one of the psychiatrists informed me that he was sorry that I had been put through this totally unwarranted examination process and that he would be making representation to Headquarters about it - most particularly to the author of the personal report from the Chief Constable's office.

Then he added something that really made my eyebrows rise. He told us of an unexplained incident that had occurred to him one evening when he was driving home from work, just as Jack had intuitively suggested.

The doctor explained how he was driving over the moors - as he did every day heading home from the hospital - when he was confronted by an object hovering about 100 meters above the road. It had the shape of a disc and it put the wind up him so much that he stepped his foot down and accelerated away as fast as he could. He did not even look back as it had really shaken him. The psychiatrist went on to say that he had never told a soul about this UFO encounter - not even his wife or any colleagues at work. Not until today!

I looked at Jack and we both looked back at the doctor and just nodded with complete understanding.

I shrugged my shoulders and told him:" *What more can I say?*" then left the room with Jack following behind.

We headed off down the long corridors towards the exit passing the previously rude 'Nurse'.

"*Byeee*" I said to her with a broad grin.

"I think your services might be needed in there!"

Indicating with my thumb the direction of the consulting room.

Out in the sunlight we made our way to the car and as I turned the recorder off Jack said:

" *Well bugger me, that was a turn up for the book.*"

I laughed and said I couldn't wait to see if the recording had worked. Once nicely seated in the car and ciggies well alight we both sat there and listened to the tape with various expressions coming across our faces as the interview went on. We both laughed because it was so weird hearing yourself caught in a conversation like this.

"That tape is dynamite, Gobber, keep it safe and sound and don't tell a bloody soul it exists, absolutely nobody, do you hear... Nobody!" Jack added.

With a knowing wink came my reply *"Ten-Four Rubber Duck, message received and understood!"*

Jack started the car up and we drove away from the hospital grounds heading back to Todmorden and home sweet home.

" *God do I need a pint Jack*" I told him grasping an imaginary glass and putting it up to my lips.

" *It's alright for you, I'm still on duty!*" He groaned.

But as we drove away from the car park the joking stopped and we both went very still, not speaking for a long time. It was only when we reached the motorway that the reality of what had just happened sank in. I had begun to get that sick feeling in my stomach as the emotional aftermath washed over me and was just about to tell Jack to pull over when he suddenly said:

" *That was all very scary. It's a good job I was with you, who knows what might have happened if you were on your own.* "

Which was exactly what I had been thinking.

Just what were the police up to with this charade? Misleading psychiatrists now and going to such extreme lengths to try to see the back of me. Was having me pronounced medically insane and suffering from hallucinations their final shot?' But if so why? I had not witnessed some political assassination attempt. It seemed so disproportionate.

Having hidden enemies plotting against me without knowing why was so frustrating. After failing to drive me out of the force by other means, now they were seeking to prove that I had lost my marbles.

"*Just watch your back please*," Jack reminded me. "*Somebody somewhere is taking no bloody prisoners!*"

It was a long drive back to Todmorden and we said very little more as we were both lost in our thoughts - stunned by what had happened and only too aware of how I might be now 'medicated' on a psych ward but for Jack being with me to intervene.

Shutting the car door behind me and giving Jack a slight nod and a thumbs up sign, I was soon inside the Red House Pub and ordering a pint with a whiskey chaser. It was to be the first of many that day!

Bet said as much with that knowing look on her face. She had sensed I was about to go on a bender. The landlady would need to keep her eye on my slow descent as I started going blotto!

I do not really remember Jack helping me out of there that night but he did. He was a very good mate and as always did his best to make sure that I was safe when the worse for wear after these sessions.

However, getting on with my normal life back at the 'Nick' would now be very hard following that examination in the hospital. So I found myself having to drink in secret just to get through another work day. I was going through packets of extra strong mints to hide the smell of alcohol on my breath but thankfully nobody on the job said anything.

Of course, I knew that if they had then I would have reached the point of no return and they would have won.

I had become wary of everybody and did not trust anyone but my closest friends. Indeed I was no longer the happy go lucky person that everyone knew me as before. My life was piece by piece unravelling around me by having to cope with these pressures. No longer joining in with any general conversations at work people started to notice and make comments about how I was keeping my distance. I would usually say I was under the weather to get them to change the subject.

In reality I was always glad to get out of the station and be away on my own, as at least then I could escape from prying eyes and questions that I did not want to answer. Not to mention fears and suspicions about who amongst them was observing me in secret and helping plot the next attempt to end my days as a copper.

On one day, a few weeks after being at the hospital, I was driving patrol when I got a call to attend at a house where a friend of the occupant could not gain access. On arrival he informed me that he was worried about the state of mind of what turned out to be his gay partner.

The couple had had an argument the previous night back at his own house and they talked about splitting up. The man was frantic, saying that his partner had taken the news badly and threatened to 'end it all' and then stormed off. Understandably he was now alarmed that he could not make contact and then arrived at the house only to find that the catch was down on the lock and the door would not even open when he used his key.

The front door of the house had a glass panel in it and, having tried all the windows first to see if we could open one of them, I decided to smash the glass to gain entry. Just to be sure I told the worried young man to stay where he was until I had searched the house. Inside I did a quick look through the downstairs rooms but having tried to switch the lights on without success I pulled back the drawn curtains.

I then made my way slowly up the steps opening the curtains back on the landing to let some light in on the darkened building.

The bathroom was empty as was the small single bedroom where curtains were already open. I then entered through the door that was ajar into the dark main upstairs room where even in the dim light I could see there wasn't anybody in the bed. So I moved over to the window and opened the curtains here and as I did so it let streams of light flow around me and I turned to be met with the horrific sight of a man hanging from the back of the bedroom door.

His knees were bent and his feet were pointing inwards and dangling. It was quickly obvious that he was dead.

Having got over the initial shock of what I was seeing I went down to inform the gentleman that – sadly - I had found the body of a man in the bedroom, but kept details from him for now. I sent for the duty doctor to attend at the house together with a scene of crimes officer from S.O.C.O. Meanwhile I secured the house and sat in the car where I took a statement from the deceased man's partner which was far from easy given that he was by now utterly distraught.

The Doctor was first to arrive and I went inside the house with him and took him to the bedroom, explaining before we entered that it was not a pretty sight.

You could be forgiven for thinking that doctors were immune from reacting to a dead body, but they are just like the rest of us and examining someone in this particular state could quite easily break you. Thankfully we all just got on with our job and the scene of crimes officer got there and had a look round to decide where to take relevant photographs for the record.

"*Pull the curtains back a bit more, to let extra light in*" he asked me.

As I obliged I heard the S.O.C.O. muttering to himself "*It's no good I will have to bring some lights in from van*" and off he went before I could say anything.

I was having a little grin to myself when he struggled back upstairs with these heavy rigs and waited until he had set them up and then said "*I hope you've brought the 'Powerpack batteries' with you*" – pointing at the light switch on the wall.

"*There's no electric*" I told him.

I followed him back to the van.

"*Give us a lift*" he pleaded.

"*These bloody things are heavy*"

He was not kidding, the battery packs were hefty constructions.

As he started taking his sad photographs of the scene, the Coroner's Carrier turned up to collect the body. It was Mick over from Hebden Bridge.

"*All right mate... What you got for me today – ow't good?*"

"*How's your stomach... Hope you haven't eaten recently?*" I told him as I helped him to take the large green body bag and case from inside the van.

" *Upstairs*" I gestured giving him a nod in that direction.

"*They are always up bloody stairs... Thoughtless.*"

"*Yes*", I replied carefully..."*But I think they might have had other things on their mind at the time than helping you.*"

After about another hour or so we were finished and I followed Mick down to the mortuary at Hebden Bridge, where we delivered the deceased and did the necessary paper work before informing the attendant and booking the Post Mortem for the following day.

Back at the 'Nick' I filled in the 'Sudden Death Report' and brought my pocket book up to date with the gruesome details of that day's events.

Before I knew it was time to clock off and a pint was drawing nearer and nearer to my lips.

It hardly touched the sides of my throat as it went down in one, followed by several more and a couple of large whisky's.

'Bet' gave me one of those looks that indicated she had picked up on my shattered mood – though, of course, I could not share the events that had just happened during my shift because the investigation was still ongoing and the details of the death were not yet public.

So to avoid awkward questions I said I was on my

way home and left.

Going home was a euphemism and really meant I was going next door to the Weavers Arms, where I could start all over again and nobody would be any the wiser. I could have two or three more pints and a couple more whisky's before actually going home.

Through this subterfuge I could consume twice as much alcohol and both worried landlords would never know the extent of my descent.

Sometimes I would even walk further up the road to the 'House that Jack Built' or even the 'Fountain' to do the same. That way nobody could keep 'tabs' on me.

Looking back now, this was the worst thing that I could have done to myself and my family. But such was the need to escape the pressures being heaped onto me at work those shadowy forces seeking to put an end to my career that I was doing this to escape from an even more terrifying reality.

I just did not want to admit that I had become an alcohol dependent man - maybe not yet quite a full out drunk but close to reaching that inevitable destination.

That realization when it finally dawned on my consciousness hit me like a brick wall.

That was probably the moment when I finally knew that I needed help… but my skill at hiding what I was doing meant nobody was looking out for me like they always had done before.

They all thought I was coping but did not see the cost of my method of doing so. Only the consequences.

I had reached crisis point and something drastic had to be done or this downward spiral I was being sucked into would fast become one from which I might never emerge.

CHAPTER NINE

Times they are a Changing

Luckily it was time for my annual Summer break and that year this meant the sun of Menorca was calling where I could relax and escape the pressures back home. Never was it more welcome. But it was going to get much hotter than the Med when I was back at the nick.

On arrival at work first day after the holiday I was eager to show off my tan but got met with an uncomfortable silence from colleagues. They seemed to be keen not to get involved with any conversation as if they knew what was going to happen but could not buck up courage to tell me.

Before long I went to my in tray and was shocked to see not just that it was empty but that my name and number had been removed from it altogether. As I stood there in the parade room I glanced through the window and the sub divisional Superintendent got out of his car and made his way towards the front door. Here was the reason for the uncomfortable silence I began to think.

The duty Inspector came into the room with a grimace across his face.

"*The Super wants to see you up in my office*" I was told gruffly.

I just nodded and brushed past him muttering under my breath to hear my boss pronounce:

"*With immediate effect PC Godfrey you are posted to Halifax so pack up your belongings from your locker and make your way over there*".

Such was the thankless manner in which I was informed of my fate they had decided during my absence.

Without transport of my own I did ask if I could be taken there with all my gear to carry but was told to '*go and catch the bus – you know the way*'.

I returned in shock to the parade room where the morning shift was about to go off duty and what should have been my colleagues that day were being assembled together with the duty Inspector.

As I made my way to pick up my belongings the Inspector said with a wicked smirk across his face:-

"*Tell me PC Godfrey how do you feel about your little move*?"

"*Actually, sir,*" I told him "*I am looking forward to working with supervisory officers with a much higher caliber than I am used to in here. It will make such a pleasant change*".

He looked at me with his mouth wide open and everybody started to laugh as they all knew, including him, that they could not do a thing about my 'insubordinate' remark now I was leaving.

I casually walked out of the room, packed my gear from the locker and left the station. I could not know then but I would only ever return one further time to a place that had been my home for so many years, but more of that later as it was another event that would have dire consequences when it happened.

Given the sudden shock I decided to go home and phone the station at Halifax and tell them I was under the weather after my trip abroad and would not be in for duty that day. They asked if I would be in the following day, which I confirmed that I would. Then I popped out and made my way down to the Red House and caught Bet just before she was about to close for the afternoon.

"*Just the one please - I won't keep you too long*".

She started to pull a pint and I told her what had just happened. Needless to say I was still there hours later. It was a good job that I was supposedly on the 2-10 pm shift so the kids were being collected by their grandad.

I felt awful when I woke up the following day but the house was empty meaning I could just get on with organizing myself and just catch the bus to Halifax. So with all my things ready I walked over to the bus station using the back streets so as not to pass Tod station and be seen by my erstwhile colleagues.

That journey to Halifax seemed to take ages and I was wondering what kind of reception awaited me. It felt strange as I arrived at the enquiry desk waiting for the duty sergeant to come and show me where to go. Already I could see that this was a very different set up. There were people constantly coming and going through the security door next to the front desk. Members of the public crowded around in the foyer waiting to speak to someone. The faster pace of this larger town felt intimidating even after years in the force.

At last the sergeant showed me to my locker and after unloading my gear I was taken to the parade room and introduced to the rest of the shift. They seemed friendly and I was just about to start up a conversation with them when the Inspector came into the room with a sergeant who told us all to fall in.

I was amused by this as we never actually had this formality back in Todmorden before we went out on duty. This station already seemed very old school by comparison as we all stood in a line whilst the Inspector checked that we had our torch, whistle, pocket book, handcuffs and truncheon.

As the sergeant made his way along our ranks and came to me he pointed at my mustache and ordered - *no facial hair below the top lip* - referring to my Mexican facial display that drooped down both sides.

"*Force Standing Orders PC Godfrey - Force Standing Orders*!" he bellowed out. " *Get that off by tomorrow Constable*".

I was gob smacked as I had had this adornment for years without issue.

So I started to fear that a change of station would not bring a change of attitude even in a place where I had no history. Perhaps word had filtered down the grapevine even this far. I was really down and depressed at the thought of years of this to come.

Happily 'Dave', the PC that had been assigned to show me round the area, changed all that, as he made me welcome and soon I was sat in one of his 'tea spots' having a brew and a fag and feeling much better.

Dave was the same kind of copper as me and I knew that I would get on with him and he would be my confidant. He introduced me to the rest of the shift as and when we bumped into them and they, too, were very friendly and the day came to an end in a more positive light than it had begun.

So I was much happier when I arrived early in Halifax for my next shift. In fact I was first there. The Inspector walked in the Parade room and the sergeant ordered us to 'Fall in' so I stood there but had not shaved the bit of hair down the side of my lips as he had ordered me to do the previous day.

The officer was shocked, but not as shocked as he was when I told him I was growing a beard as per 'Standing Orders' permitting me to do. He sent me down to the cell block to work where, as he put it, I could 'reflect on my decision'

I enjoyed working at Halifax. That Inspector eventually became a frequent visitor to the cells and my good friend. In due course we would laugh about those first couple of days and he used to say that I reminded him of himself when he first started on the beat.

This inspector stood head and shoulders above those back in Tod and that became all too clear when I had to return to my old posting for a court date.

That appearance was a couple of months after my transfer to Halifax and involved a case I had worked on before leaving. Of course, I still lived in Todmorden - not far from the police station - but it felt very strange entering the old building to prepare for court. It looked small and dingy inside as I had got used to the much larger premises in Halifax with its bigger complement of officers. But the unfriendly atmosphere I recalled from here had not defrosted.

Nobody spoke to me so I just picked up my files and made my way on foot down to the court room which was situated in the large town hall in the middle of Tod. On the way there in full uniform I passed the open market and spoke to lots of people who asked me where I had been all these weeks, which was nice to know that at least members of the public had missed me.

After the court hearing I returned to the station and had a fish and chip dinner that I had bought on the way and then got into the car that I had recently bought and drove over to Halifax to start my 2-10 shift.

Only after I got there did I realize that I had left my helmet back at Todmorden nick so from my office in Halifax I phoned PC Lindsay who had just come on duty in Tod and he informed me that my helmet was indeed still there so he would leave it in the control room for me to pick up on my way home that night.

Sadly, after a full day in Halifax, I simply forgot about calling in, which turned out to be a big mistake.

Some weeks later I finished my shift and dashed back to Todmorden in time to catch the Red House pub open. Bet started to pull me a pint when she said:

" *What's all this about you being barred from the station? Is it anything to do with being moved down to Halifax?*"

"*What are you on about, Bet?*" I asked....*Barred from Tod nick?...Who's told you that?*"

" *The lads over there*" she said - pointing to a group of my ex bobby mates from the Todmorden shift .

Walking over to them with my pint in hand I said with a chuckle:

" *Okay then lads - what's all this nonsense about me being barred from the nick?*" – fully expecting them to start laughing after teasing Bet with this joke.

The look on their faces and their eyes staring gloomily in silence or at their feet made me suspect that they were really being serious.

I stood there quietly for a few minutes wondering what was going on before I asked them pointedly.

" *Come on - .tell me what's happened. Bet says I have been barred from Tod Nick ...Is that right or is it just a wind up?*"

One of the lads said that the duty Inspector - who

just happened to be the same one that instigated my move to Halifax - along with the duty Sergeant - had called a parade at changeover time with both the 6am-2pm and the 2pm-10pm shifts and informed everyone that from this date forward PC Godfrey was officially barred from entering the Police Station because things had been reported missing during his presence.

"If he comes in you will ask him to leave and if he refuses you should inform me or the Sergeant and we will remove him ourselves," they stated.

I was gob smacked on hearing this allegation - *things going missing* and I was *barred from the Nick*?' What on Earth was such nonsense?

After a long discussion with the lads I supped my pint and went home where I sat thinking what might happen when I returned on duty at Halifax the following morning.

To say that I did not sleep well that night is an understatement as my head was all over the place and I was in no better mood the following morning. But I had decided to face it all head on when I reported for duty.

On arriving for my shift at Halifax I went straight in to see my Inspector who was shocked to hear what had happened. He phoned the Chief Superintendent Head of the Halifax Division to make me an appointment to see him without disclosing the reason. It was obvious that he did not like the way I was being treated by the officers at Todmorden. I was then informed that I could go straight round to Divisional Headquarters - which I did.

There are times when you just have to go with your head held high and say exactly what you think. And this was one of them. Whatever had been going on back at my old station, even if I had spoken out of line once or twice as I had, the consequences were now out of all proportion.

I gave the Chief Super the story and he was shocked by the anger with which I spoke but I was beyond caring by this point. After all the other things these innuendos that I was a thief were now totally unacceptable.

The Super said he had no knowledge of any such events back in Todmorden but would look into it. I told him he could do what he liked but enough was enough for me and I was not going to just sit back whilst unknown persons in the force were treating me like this. I was going to take legal advice and if I needed to do so would be taking the matter into my own hands via the courts. Whoever they were I could not let them besmirch my good name. Saying I was mentally ill had been bad enough. But to accuse someone of being a thief was about the worst thing you could do to a police officer.

Things now took on a real pace. I spoke to UFO researcher Harry Harris in his capacity as a solicitor and he soon got an appointment with a barrister in Manchester and took statements from some of the officers who were on that Parade and heard these accusations of theft. It was clear from their statements that they were in no doubt that I was being accused of stealing though details were never explained to them.

Harry also took statements from members of the public who had heard about me being barred and then got all the paperwork sorted and applied for writs to be issued at the Queens Bench Division High Court Manchester. I them made another appointment to see the Divisional Commander in Halifax.

I gave the commander copies of these statements and informed him that I was willing to wait for police Internal Affairs to investigate before deciding what action I would take. But if I was not satisfied with the outcome of that internal investigation I would have no choice but to go to court to clear my name.

Months passed without reply and when I spoke to some officers who had provided written statements for me they now explained that pressure had been brought from above since they signed. They needed to withdraw those from the record or at best dilute their words. Happily a few were so angered by those demands that they gave me new statements adding this threat to what they had written before.

Armed with these allegations I again went to see the Divisional Commander and implored him to get to the bottom of what was going on and gave a week for internal affairs to report back or my solicitor would be told to file suit. Though little did I know whilst all of this was going on a more dastardly plan was being hatched somewhere to ‘fit me up’ good and proper.

Just before the week ended I was in my office in the cells at Halifax Police Station when I got a visit from Internal Affairs. I was relieved that they had finally decided to investigate my complaints after weeks of doing nothing. But they were actually there to investigate me instead!

They told me somberly that an item of uniform - a police helmet - had gone missing from Todmorden on the date that I attended my court hearing.

I was dumb struck by this allegation and pointed out that I had indeed left my own helmet there on that date by accident and was supposed to get it on my way home from Halifax but forgot. But when I had spoken to PC Lindsay to apologise and arranged another time to pick it up Lindsay told me that the helmet had been found in the cellar of the police station 'ripped to bits by persons unknown'. I had never bothered to retrieve those remains, assuming it was one of my 'friends' in Tod who was being petty.

Now all this might seem trivial to the reader but the two officers from Internal Affairs looked thoroughly bemused over my account. When I brought up the subject of my being banned from Todmorden nick for this 'theft' they said they weren't here to look into that claim – just the 'missing helmet' - and got up and left.

This just confirmed what I had suspected all along that nothing was being investigated regarding my own complaints or any effort made to find out who was behind the seemingly unending vendetta at Tod. So when they left I phoned Harry and told him to go ahead with the writs. It seemed the only way to get to the truth.

A couple of weeks went by before I heard back that I would have to deposit a surety of several thousand pounds into the High Court before I could go ahead with issuing a writ. Of course I didn't have that kind of money and I could not risk my house with family and a new child on the way. In today's terms the sum I was being asked to find was huge and well outside my pay grade. So I approached the Police Federation, which had a local office in Wakefield, and went there for a meeting hoping to find an amicable resolution outside of court.

Sadly, they preferred not to get 'involved' in what the local representative termed a 'dispute'. I came home bitterly disappointed by their attitude. I was being treated like some sort of criminal and the federation did not seem to want to help one of their own clear his name against egregious and clearly fallacious slurs.

As days passed I felt that I was being boxed into a corner. So in disgust I resigned from the Police Federation the following day and I was now truly out on my own and would have to fight on without support. But fears grew that a prison cell might even be my next home if I persisted in my quest for justice.

Meanwhile, I had been getting on with my Halifax post as best I could - still happily on the outside of cells at Harrison Road Police Station - when a night arrived that yet again defied credibility.

At about 2am on late shift the front desk PC, whom I shall call 'Bob', came in the cells for his meal break as he often did when we were working nights. He sat down and I made us a brew. We chatted away whilst eating our 'snap' discussing everything under the sun to try to put the world to right.

Bob then told me about a plain clothes officer whom he had not recognised. The man had entered the station and showed a warrant card and asked to be admitted which, of course, Bob allowed. The stranger then asked where the Inspectors office was and Bob told him that he was out on patrol in the car. The plain clothes man had nodded and then asked where the lockers were situated. Without thinking much about this request Bob had told him.

The visitor said that he would wait for the Inspector to return and he and Bob parted company. But as we carried on chatting I started to get a bad feeling about this story and decided not to let on to Bob about my misgivings until he revealed that the plain clothes officer had left about 10mins after this conversation and oddly without waiting for the Inspector to return.

I remarked that this was strange and asked Bob what he thought the man might have been up to. Bob just shrugged and went back to work at the front desk.

So who was this visitor and why was he interested in where the lockers were located? Was I being silly to think it was anything to do with me? I decided to stop fretting and just go have a quick look at the lockers to see if anything was awry. A natural coppers instinct for trouble, perhaps. But thank goodness for it.

When I arrived at my locker everything seemed to be fine until I inserted the key and turned it and the lock on the inside fell off with a clang. I could see that inside there was now a police helmet on the top shelf where there was not one before when I had last opened it.

Then as I pulled it out to see whose helmet it was (realising that it was not mine) two small see through packages fell to the floor from within. I picked them up and inside both there was a white powder which looked very suspicious indeed.

I was in a state of total shock but had to think very fast on my feet. So I put the packets into my pocket and had a look at the helmet. I recognised who it belonged to and could not understand why it was anywhere near – let alone in - my locker so I put it on top of another locker a long way down the room and headed back to the cells.

As my route took me past the desk I asked Bob what the plain clothes officer who visited earlier had looked like and if had he noticed the man's name when he showed his warrant card to gain entry? Sadly he hadn't.

From the description Bob offered I knew straight away this visitor was the 'Man from the Ministry'. But I decided not to let on that I recognised him nor mention the terrifying details of what someone had placed inside my locker after I had arrived on shift and during the time when this man had been there and asked where to find the lockers.

I was too stunned to think straight. Why would someone even consider doing something as dreadful as this to me?

This was now far beyond trying to discredit my UFO story. Someone seemed desperate to get me charged and arrested for a serious criminal offence.

As soon as I got back to the cells I made my way to the toilets and flushed the mysterious contents of both those packages down the bog and wondered what those hidden forces would dare to attempt next.

My kids might even be in their sights I realised with horror. It was now close to the point of no return.

Back home I could not sleep at all as this event had terrified me. It was horrifying to know that someone was willing and powerful enough to be able to go to such lengths just to 'get' rid of me.

In desperation I phoned Jack later that day and we arranged to meet. I told him what had happened and he calmed me down and we went over different scenarios of what I might encounter when I went back on duty.

We concluded that if there was nothing in my locker now that I had removed it then nobody could do anything. He advised me to just act normal and be surprised if they searched my locker because we both knew that I was innocent and everything would be fine.

It was a long day waiting to go back on my next night shift but I picked up my Dictaphone recorder and set it to record before I left. I knew I needed evidence in this situation more than ever so was taking no chances over disputes about who said what and when.

On the way to work I picked up my mate as usual and we spoke very little. Even so it became clear he was not going to say anything about what had happened unless absolutely forced to do so. I understood his reticence, of course – his job was on the line as well as mine if he backed me up - but it meant that I really was out on my own.

I parked the car and we made our way into the station where I was met at the front desk by a uniformed Sergeant not from our station but from Divisional Headquarters which I knew was unusual. Two plain clothes officers from Internal affairs were also with him - an Inspector and a Sergeant.

My mate walked straight past me and said nothing. Instinctively I put my hand in my pocket and pressed the record button on my tape machine as my sergeant spoke.

"PC Godfrey - these two officers want to conduct a search of your locker as they have reason to believe that there are items in there that do not belong to you"

I replied, trying to keep calm - *"Items such as what exactly?"*

" A police helmet belonging to an officer from Todmorden that went missing on the day when you attended court there."

I remained in control as I answered: "*I haven't got a clue what you are on about but, of course, you can have a look if you want.*"

So off we went in full gaze of other officers milling around the station. As we got there you could see there was a small hole in the door where the front of the lock should have been and I made a point of reporting that fact to them.

I opened the door and surprise, surprise nothing was in there except for what should have been - my tunic and raincoat. I knew how narrowly I had escaped.

What happened next took me by surprise as the Inspector started to search my tunic pockets. So I grabbed his arm and said: "*Why are you going through my pockets? You won't find a missing helmet in there*".

I added bluntly: "*What the hell is going on here? I am going to make an official complaint to the Chief Constable about this.*"

They all left without further explanation.

I went down to my office in the cells and quickly switched the play back on my Dictaphone and every word had recorded clearly confirming what had just taken place. I had another piece of evidence as back-up if required and I was already prepared to take the matter up personally with the Chief Constable and tape my meeting with him, too, if that proved necessary.

After a bit of phoning around I had now got a collection of times and dates and the names of the officers that were witness to this saga over the past two days so that I could get them all to tell me what happened and what was said. I did so without raising suspicion that I was recording them secretly at the same time. I hated doing this covertly to my colleagues but was being forced into this desperate act out of self-preservation.

You might think that my tactics were rather underhand but my colleagues telling me to my face what they saw or heard was one thing and them doing so after being interviewed by Internal Affairs or the Chief was a different ball game as I had seen back in Tod. When pressure was put on by the ruthless folk who seemed to be after me these officers would be urged to 'deny or forget' and to protect their jobs no doubt some would.

So I could not just hope they would put their careers on the line for someone they had only just met and now being accused of all sorts of bizarre things after starring in the tabloids for abduction by 'little green men'.

Given what I had been through in the last couple of years my only option was to record these conversations in case they were needed to preserve my liberty.

The interviews were made with each officer across several months but once I got that far I was ready to see the Chief Constable and present all of my complaints.

I was preparing this when I spoke with Jenny Randles and arranged a meeting to consider how these events might affect the book we had been working on. She was horrified to discover the extent to which my story had spiraled out of control as she had only heard a small fraction of them through her family connections.

Months went by and I still had not made an appointment to see the Chief Constable as I had become wrapped up with Jenny's investigation and the forth coming book. So I put it on 'back burner.

Then one evening when I was on nights I had a visit in my office from a plain clothes officer from 'Internal Affairs' but not one I had met before. There had been no warning of his visit and I dared to hope that at last they were investigating my complaint.

But to my surprise he started asking me about Jenny Randles and the book she was publishing and my involvement in what was soon to appear from Granada as 'The Pennine UFO Mystery'.

I cracked on that I had no idea what he was talking about but he would not leave it at that so I threatened to speak to my Solicitor if he carried on harassing me. I did so bearing in mind that the force were by now fully aware that I had taken legal advice concerning what had gone on at Todmorden nick. Luckily after that comment he backed off and left. But the fact he was aware of our ongoing cooperation was most revealing.

The book was in stores in Summer 1983 and sold its first print quickly but was never reprinted. Jenny tells me that it has remained the most widely requested of her 50 books to date because it was so hard to find. She had not even been able to buy copies to sell herself as authors often do because none were left to buy.

Soon after the book appeared I was not thinking of such matters because terrible events happened once again that would re-direct my entire future forever.

I was working night shift down the cells when a young teenager was brought in under arrest for assault. He was 'high' from glue sniffing and as strong as an ox. As we attempted to take him to the cells he lashed out and hit one of the arresting officers and then viciously kicked me in the groin. I toppled like a tree.

He had caught me in the area of my multiple previous operations and I was in agony again. I was rushed to hospital and for a couple of nights they evaluated my injuries before transferring me to Burnley Hospital where the same surgeon who had operated before was forced to open me up again.

Recovery this time was slow and took many weeks and I was informed by the force during recuperation that I would now need a medical before they would consider my return to duty. Just to ensure that I was fit and proper for service, you understand, they said, of course.

Immediately I feared that after all their failed attempts this latest misfortune would provide the perfect excuse for them to get rid of me once and for all.

In due course I attended the force surgeon who to no great surprise deemed this time it was too much of a risk for me to return to duty and that it was best I accept my notice on those grounds preserving my benefits and my respect.

I was devastated and appealed the decision because I loved the job but it was unsuccessful and a date was set for me to leave.

The powers-that-be had tried so many ways to bring me down using dastardly methods, but in the end two assaults whilst doing my duty as a police officer did what years of underhand tactics could not.

Those smears and lies and efforts to say I suffered hallucinations did not bring me down. Nor the attempt to frame me for a crime. It was two thugs who by chance targeted a vulnerable part of my anatomy.

With Jenny's book getting media attention and my case in the public eye once more I suddenly got an invitation to appear on BBC Breakfast Time in London. There had been many similar requests before but I turned them all down whilst I was a serving officer. After what had happened when I spoke to the press under direct police orders I felt it was unwise to give them another excuse to claim I was bringing the force into disrepute.

But now I thought, what the hell, if you have to leave a job you love then why not go out in a blaze of glory in front of a million viewers!

So that is exactly what I did.

You would not believe the uproar it caused when I got back to the station after my live appearance to the nation. It was basically me just sticking two fingers up to those shady forces who believed they could control me.

But was I bothered? What do you think?

I did get one final chance to air my complaints with the Chief when he agreed to meet me to discuss why I had been asked to 'retire'.

On that meeting I told him everything that had gone on over the years assuming he was largely unaware of these facts. He listened but had no solution to offer to the many questions that I posed.

But he did comment about the forces and events that had shaped my life and that had now collided to end my career in the police.

'*Who or what were they?*' He asked me all too pointedly.

From whom or where did those mysterious forces take orders to bring me down and why was it so important to somebody to try all they could to discourage me from telling *you* the truth?

These are very good questions for which I am still seeking answers.

A week or two after visiting the Chief I went down to Halifax to hand in my uniform and warrant card. It was such a sad day given my love of the job.

I went to see my old Inspector who shook my hand and wished me all the best. He told me how disappointed he was to see me leave and I thanked him in return for his support since my arrival from Tod 2 years earlier. We laughed about the incident on that first parade concerning my 'tash' and I left to go up to the control room to say my goodbyes to the rest of the crew.

Whilst there – Dick - one of the lads – asked if I was having a retirement do. I hadn't really thought about this up to now, but said: " Why not?"

So plans were set in motion.

Back in Tod I went to the Red House to ask Bet if she could organise something at the pub. She was delighted to agree. I had been to another officers retirement party held here and it was a good night. Bet said that she would put in for an extension of licensing hours for that night as she had done successfully on such occasions before. So we had a couple of drinks together and agreed a date before I made my way home.

I then started to organise transport for the lads to travel over from Halifax so they could drink and not have to worry about how to get home late at night. I saw Graham Lindsay, my old tutor constable, and good friend, and asked if he would put up a notice in Tod nick inviting any of the lads from my old workplace to come as well and he happily agreed.

During the next week I met some of those Todmorden bobbies socially in the Red House and gave them a personal invitation. But it became clear from their replies that they had been warned off from attending by that local Inspector – the one that I had crossed swords with too many times.

To the bitter end he would be seeking his revenge.

So I just told the lads - the invite stands it's up to you.

Bet then came back to me and reported that the Inspector had been in the pub to see her and informed that Tod police would officially object to her application to extend hours. She asked me what I wanted to do.

I told her not to worry as it was a routine application and I would go to the court and speak to the magistrates directly. So when the date came to hear what was a frequently approved application process I went to court and was surprised that instead of the usual sergeant on license application duty it was my old nemesis – the Inspector - determined to stop this one dead.

There were several applications from various pubs before ours came up and the Inspector then rose to his feet and informed the bench that the police were opposing this application on the grounds that they did not want the public to think that favouritism was being shown to a retiring officer by granting an extension.

What a bizarre thing to say to the magistrates and, unsurprisingly, the chairman rebuked him for even thinking that anyone would see a form of favouritism in an innocent request that got approved more often than not when applications were reasonable. He asked if there was a representative for the hostelry in court.

At that point I raised my hand and was asked to step into the witness box. But as I gave my name and took the oath I could see the Inspector's face – it was in shock and he had no idea that I was present until that moment.

After some questions from the Inspector about 'Supper hour Licenses' I reminded the court that the application was an extension of hours for a retirement party. The inspector looked rather flummoxed as the chairman asked how long the pub wanted this to run and I explained to 1am with half an hour for drinking up. The magistrate chair nodded as it was perfectly normal.

A look like thunder then came onto the Inspector's face when the chairman said calmly that, as many of the guests were coming over from Halifax and would not finish duty shift until 10pm, he would allow and, indeed, voluntarily extend the application by another hour to 2am with half an hour further for drinking up time!

I left the court with a grin from ear to ear and made my way to the Red House to give Bet the good news.

The party went ahead as planned and at its close there was not one glass of beer to be seen because we were very keen to abide by the letter of the law given the large number of coppers on the premises.

However, the place was full with people bidding farewells and preparing to take trides back home when a uniformed Sergeant and two PCs from Tod station walked in and demanded to check everyone present. They marched through the pub looking carefully for anything incriminating but found absolutely nothing.

As they left the Sergeant said very apologetically:

"I am so sorry Alan but orders are orders. Carry on. We won't be back. Have a good night."

In contrast to this extraordinary pettiness from the higher ranks at Todmorden the lads from Halifax were fantastic and presented me with an inscribed carriage clock before we left that night. The inscription read:

'To Alan from his mates at Harrison Road Nick '

I was moved by their respect and gave a somewhat merry speech but cannot remember what I said or even if it was intelligible. But it was sad that only a couple of lads from Todmorden nick braved 'advice' from that inspector not to be attend. The rest heeded his warning and, given how they saw what happened to me, I cannot blame them - though it hurt a lot at the time.

All I did during my years working for West Yorkshire Police was try to perform my duty and honestly report what happened even when it would have been easier to lie or look the other way.

Where UFOs are concerned it would seem that someone behind the thin blue line or in a dark corner of a shadow department felt that telling it straight must not be allowed. Forces decreed that you - the public - do not deserve to hear these facts, weigh them up and decide for yourselves what happened.

Instead they did what they could to discredit me with increasingly dark methods straight out of a crime thriller. And on every occasion their nefarious tactics failed – because truth in the end was the victor.

Of course, exactly what truth means - in so far as the things that happened to me on Burnley Road - must be up to you to decide. I wish you luck as I have been trying to find those answers for 37 years.

POSTSCRIPT

BACK TO THE FUTURE

Many years have passed since I walked out of police headquarters and the job that I loved. I was only 27 years old when I had joined the force and now I am 70 and so much water has flowed under the bridge.

I started to write this book over 25 years ago but never really expected to be able to finish it, let alone see it published. So I am grateful to my friend, Jenny Randles, who has put in many hours helping me make this dream become possible. Otherwise it might never have seen the light of day.

But now that it is finished I have been able to review my own story from start to finish in the form of a book instead of just a collection of notes written down by me at various times over the years. This has brought home to me the full extent of how I was mistreated.

To tell the truth it really hurts me deep inside even to this day. It was not just a case of those people trying to get rid of me and the tactics that they used. Such things were bad enough, of course. But the relentlessness of the assault on my character that nearly destroyed me as a human being. Those shameless people drove me to the edge of sanity and almost succeeded in pushing me over the top. That should never have happened and, I want to believe that it would not be allowed in today's police service.

So what did the future hold after my journey to the beyond and back? Did it turn out as bad as I had feared or were my concerns unfounded?

I have had many questions asked of me over those years by reporters and ordinary folk intrigued by what happened - but the main one has been:

"Would you still have reported the UFO if you had known how much trouble it would cause you personally and that it would cost you your job?"

The answer to that is very simple. No - I would not have reported the incident had I had known how it would end. That is sad and makes me wonder about others who might be in a similar predicament.

But it is too easy to speak in hindsight as we all must act at the time according to our conscience.

So what was done was done and the bad things did have a major upside. They enabled me in later years to help raise thousands of pounds for charity by giving talks about my encounter. I can look back upon this with pride as a positive outcome from a traumatic experience.

I have also met some very famous people because

of my sighting - including the second man to step on the moon - Buzz Aldrin - when we both appeared on the Frank Skinner TV show together. It was such a thrill when I had a long chat with him in the green room.

We had something quite unusual in common – two men who had boldly gone where few others have gone before. Though in my case exactly where I less than boldly went is still unclear.

Mind you, I also made a booboo by not knowing who rock star Bon Jovi was when we met and so failing to get his autograph for my daughter, Julie. I nearly needed a ride on an Apollo rocket to get out of that one.

So, yes it has been a long and winding road with many up's and down's, but I have come out of the other side knowing that I did the right thing whatever the cost in terms of my personal life and my job. As a copper you learn that you can never put a price on telling the truth.

I am still convinced that Adamski did not die where his body was found and in both the opinion of PC Malcolm Agley and myself - whether his demise was from a criminal act or something else - we will likely never know.

The question I have always asked myself is: - *Why would a man who has never visited Todmorden arrive in a location that most people who live there have probably not been and then climb up a stack of wet, slick coal with a heart condition just to lie on his back with arms across his chest and face death with eyes wide open?*

Then you must wonder why - if he was put there by someone – they would place him at the top of that coal heap at risk of being seen in daylight and likely soon discovered? If you were trying to hide a body then you would put it out of sight so as not to be found before you make your escape.

These are questions that nobody has yet been able to answer.

The other thing that I have always asked myself is - Why did a Chief Constable allow what happened to continue to happen *if* he was aware of what was going on enough to say what he did on that final meeting?

He seemed to feel that 'others' should have let sleeping dogs lie - but *what* others? This takes us full circle to the questions posed at the start of this book :

"Who or what were they?"

Who?

This is the easy part for me, because I know who the officers were that plotted against me and more to the point so do they. I have not named them here because I did not need to.

I hope that some of those who did these things have the courage to read this book and face up to some regret. They should realise that they were not just engaging in a petty vendetta but went too far. Whatever the reason they thought that they must act as they did then this could not explain the extent of their actions.

Yes I was a copper under their command, but also a human being and there can be no justification for acting like that with anyone.

So I hope they feel ashamed and can perhaps look back with a more moderate perception brought by the passage of years. I know that I would if I had done those things to someone else.

What ?

Let me start with the 'Man from the Ministry'. Was he really from some Whitehall department - MI5 or MI6? I do not think so. Was he from the Ministry at all?

Jenny tells me she investigated a report from Wilmslow in Cheshire after doubting the solution reached by researchers at the time who felt that it was just a bright meteor. Jodrell Bank – to where it was reported by the witness – did not agree and nor did Jenny. So she traced the witness and interviewed him 30 years later, found that a local woman had also described the same thing on that night and – most importantly – that the Ministry of Defence held a secret file about the case. What seemed a simple misperception had hidden depths.

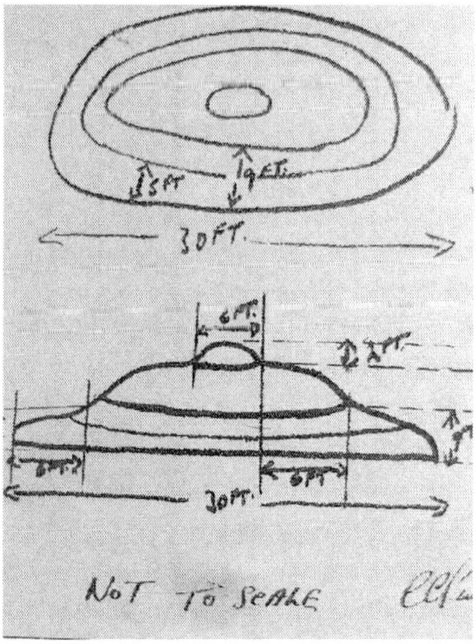

The witness was a 28 year old police constable – Colin Perks. He was on the 10 pm – 6 am shift (same as I was) at a town now beloved by footballers and TV celebs. At 4.10 am on 7 January 1966 he saw the object as drawn by him in the sketch over page hovering near an electricity sub-station. He described it as the 'size of a bus' and 35 feet off the ground glowing green-grey.

At first the object was still but had a solid structure. Then it flew away at speed south eastward making a high pitched whining noise throughout. When he returned to the nick the lads on his shift cracked jokes about Daleks but his supervising officer knew his shock was for real and submitted an official file to the Ministry. He was made aware of his signature to the Official Secrets Act and told not to talk just as I was and so never revealed what happened next until free to do so.

In 1997 his file was declassified by the Ministry of Defence. It revealed he was visited on 1 February 1966 by a bona fide 'man from the ministry' – a Flight Lieutenant Mercer of a defence intelligence unit. Unable to solve the case that report was impressed by the witness saying there was '*no reason to doubt'* that PC Perks saw something *'completely foreign to his previous experience.*' Mercer even scoured the location seeking physical evidence and sent some glassy substance found on the ground for lab analysis. It was never identified.

So in this case with many comparisons to my own we do have documented proof that the MoD *did* visit covertly, but I still have doubts that this happened with me. I think my 'man' might have been a plain clothes inspector from internal affairs trying to put the wind up with grandiose claims when I signed that 'Minute' and was 'reminded' about the Official Secrets Act.

Maybe I fell for that ruse but on looking back it was quite possibly just to deter me from talking freely. That said, I have spoken often in public about my sighting and Adamski since signing that minute sheet so I would be doing about 10 life sentences by now if it was a genuine threat and not just a scare tactic.

Why?

I realise that I may never know the answer to the ultimate question. Why did all of these things happen as they did? Perhaps you have your own thoughts and I would love to hear them from you (see page 316).

In any case you must judge if what I did throughout this story was right. I imagine I did not always handle everything perfectly as human beings all have our strengths and weaknesses. But I sincerely believe that I at least tried to do the right thing.

After reading this book you may come to your own conclusions about what really happened on Burnley Road that night in November 1980. Did I see a UFO from another world or did something else occur?

I know what my answer was at the time and as the years have flown by events have not changed my impression that I saw a physical craft of some kind from somewhere. But where that somewhere was I do not know.

The hypnosis sessions that I underwent with Professor Blair and Dr Jaffee never resolved things further. What I said whilst regressed sits in my mind as a strange adventure alongside my actual memory.

Is that part of my story fact or fiction or a mixture of the two? There is no way to be sure, but I do know for an absolute fact that I saw that UFO above Burnley Road and it *was* a real object. It was in my headlights reflecting light and left tangible marks on the road underneath. That is about as real as you can get.

The story that emerged from hypnosis is also true up to the point where that bright light 'hit' me whilst I sketched the object because it simply sharpened my recall of real events around that point. These were also verified by others who were out there that night.

But as for the rest – such as being taken aboard and examined by the tall being called 'Yosef' and the eight small creatures with lamp shaped heads - did they really exist? Or was this a story created by my mind playing tricks and perhaps resulting from that book about UFOs someone lent to me before the sessions began?

I know I really did have a small round red mark on my left instep afterwards and the boot that I was wearing had a split across the sole. Jenny's photograph of this (see page 107) shows that really happened. The marks left on Burnley Road were real, too. But does any of this prove that I was abducted into a craft hovering above?

I don't know, because I have no *conscious* memory of that part. Even 37 years later that story is only what I said under hypnosis. Both doctors who unearthed it under hypnosis were convinced that something happened to me that night and it caused me great anxiety. Indeed the physical aftermath reveals that this is true. So, real or not, these 'experiences' were emotionally overpowering.

But could that anxiety result from the stress of the sighting itself or was it coming from an inner awareness of something deep in my mind that I know also happened but am trying to repress?

Are these tantalising glimpses of extraordinary events inside the UFO genuine pointers to a hidden truth or a strange kind of imagining built around my darker fears of what might have happened?

For now, this is all that I can say and you must ponder the meaning behind my words and reach your own conclusion.

Since my encounter and during the writing of this account I have been helped by someone who has been one of the tiny few full time researchers into the UFO mystery over the past 40 years and written books and presented documentaries for TV and radio. She has investigated cases similar to my own around the world and lectured at universities, RAF bases and even a House of Lords group formed to discuss UFOs in Westminster involving serious political figures.

Jenny has kindly agreed to share her thoughts about my case based on this experience of UFO investigation. She will reveal how MUFORA - the Manchester team of researchers mentioned throughout this book and that she was part of - looked hard for an explanation and show some of the twists and turns and possibilities this search for answers considered across the years.

Hopefully, Jenny's insights into how UFO researchers delve into these strange things will surprise you and show some unexpected things that are taken into account during investigation of this subject.

This is not UFO investigation as you might imagine from the tabloids – wide eyed believers chasing shadows and desperate to convince the world of cosmic conspiracies. It is a genuine quest to find serious answers.

Also - as shown by the recent appearance of a new witness on Burnley Road on that night - I think this may still be an ongoing story that is not quite done yet. Who knows where the search will eventually lead?

But whatever you decide after reading this book hopefully there *will* be a resolution at some point.

If and when we find that truth then the ultimate conclusion will have stretched from a wet winter highway in Todmorden all the way to who knows where?

Alan Godfrey, October 2017

Afterword

Jenny Randles

Those Things Up in the Sky

Reports of alien abduction form less than one in a thousand cases. But so many UFO sightings occur around the world each year that we still have a few thousand accounts of where people see a UFO along with their presumed occupants.

Several hundred cases, some well documented, are on record from the UK and Alan Godfrey's is the most important of its kind. Out of about 20 such cases that I have investigated over the past 40 years it is the only British example that made top rankings in a global list drawn up by some of the main experts on the subject.

In 1991 I was honoured to be British representative of researchers, scientists, folklorists and psychologists who spent a week at the prestigious MIT (Massachusetts Institute of Technology) - near Boston - debating how to handle 'close encounters'. Alan's case was something I was asked about there. It is high time that he got this chance to tell the full disturbing story first hand.

I advised those at MIT what I do to you now. Alan is a very trustworthy witness. If he says he saw something, then I believe him. Figure out what happened on that night and it will take us a long way towards understanding this extraordinary global enigma.

Yet questions abound. Do we take these reports at face value and conclude that an alien intelligence is contacting mankind? If so, then why are they here?

Or is there another way to understand them without implying that these witnesses are just making it up? Because I believe that we owe to those brave souls more than knowing winks when their backs are turned. They deserve respect from us to match their sincerity.

It could be you whose life is turned upside down tomorrow by a UFO. As a society we can surely do more than shrug our shoulders declining to investigate. Because, if it *was* you then you would rightly expect us to look for answers rather than glibly cast aspersions.

In my childhood during the 1960s I often wandered the moors around Bacup and Tod, as my granddad pointed out places from family history and we gazed at 'those things up in the sky'. This is what he called the oft reported strange lights seen in these parts and I wrongly assumed then that they were all stars.

Born into the small valley community of Stacksteads a quarter mile from where Mike Sacks had his encounter it became easy to imagine that aliens might view these hills as a haven. Mike had called Jodrell Bank to report an odd light in 1978 and they gave him my number to follow through. As a result he was able to phone me live weeks later to describe the landing in the quarry as it happened. He is not the only one in Rossendale to have seen UFOs in that nearby valley.

My first direct brush with those 'things' had come in August 1963 when staying with my Stacksteads grandparents in Blackpool near the pier. As a pre-teen I was in bed by that late hour, but recall residents reporting next day the lights seen over our roof. Some had even gone to observe a pink orb that seemed to land.

My grandmother told me when I was a little older that it happened but would never elaborate.

Back in 1979 as I started to investigate Mike's UFO landing in that quarry (one where my gran's father had even once worked) a security guard from that same pier in Blackpool approached me at a lecture. On the night of Mike's 'landing' this guard had been working on that pier and in his tea break reading a story in Titbits magazine titled '*close encounter with Britain's UFO Girl'* – this story being about me!

Even as he read that article the UFO that Mike had watched pass above the spot where I was born now rattled this pier with a fighter jet behind. The metalwork shook as it dipped beneath the Irish Sea and a circle closed in a cosmic symphony riddled with coincidence.

It is tempting to see hidden forces shuffling human chess pieces in things such as this. The UFO mystery can be weird like that. Certainly we should not ignore any possibility, however bizarre. But we also need to anchor ourselves in common sense to be sure that our imagination does not run amok, as it can so easily do.

As I became a full time investigator of UFOs in the late 1970s the first thing I learned about them is how the acronym gets misunderstood. It stands for 'Unident*ified* Flying Object' – nothing more. Yet around 95% ***do*** have explanations. They are often obvious such as meteors or fire lanterns and odder things still, like shape changing clouds of toxic fumes or stars distorted by a mirage like effect akin to how on hot days a phantom pool of water forms by refracting the sky onto the highway ahead. Hundreds of different things have caused UFO sightings.

So, yes, most UFO reports turn out to become IFOs – *Identified* Flying Objects – if you investigate them well. And when I was supervising the national network at the British UFO Research Association – I used to ask investigators to regard finding an explanation a success – not a failure - because that is really what our job should be about. To reveal to a witness what they saw, if possible, and put their minds at rest over events that can be very unsettling. Though, of course, also accept that sometimes there simply is no answer.

I recall a terrified woman who met me in the supermarket. She had seen a hovering UFO behind her garden late one night and was afraid that it might come back to snatch her child. To be able to find an explanation (it was a helicopter on a survey mission using a searchlight) gave her peace of mind. After seeing this obvious relief I never again considered solving any case to be a disappointment.

Yet resolving 95% of cases is not the same thing as removing them all from being remarkable. An investigators job is to document facts so that reasonable conclusions either way can be reached. And that means sometimes you will be left with a genuine mystery.

Another common misperception is that the term UFO is just a synonym for *alien spaceship* – so if you see something weird up in the sky then – if you are not merely puddled - you must have inevitably encountered little green men in their flying machines.

Well, sadly, no you haven't. It is not that simple. After you eliminate the 95% that are IFOs the remainder are just unresolved things. We should not presume more than that.

For instance, after 40 years of research I have concluded that some of the puzzling sightings involve forces latent within our atmosphere which we might learn to harness in the same way as we can now tame the wind or electricity. And I suspect this may be why governments and defence agencies worldwide have had an abiding interest throughout the decades.

It is not as oft assumed because they have proof we have been invaded by aliens or bodies locked in hangars but because they suspect some UFOs might involve energies that could be used for economic advantage or, sadly as likely, to build weapons. Governments cannot ignore this possibility in case enemies are researching the same option. This may be why 'the ministry' was so concerned about Alan's contacts with Russia.

Most of the real knowledge we have gained on UFOs by investigation across the years lacks the X factor that headline hungry tabloids desire. So here is one missing headline you might not have seen. There are areas around the world where powerful forces concentrate and trigger 'storms' of UFOs. We call them 'Window Areas' and there is a long record of people seeing 'things up in the sky' in these hotspots.

One of the best studied windows is a remote area of Norway - the Hessdalen valley - where scientific expeditions have used sophisticated equipment to brave the ice and observe, track and photograph glowing UFOs. Their data indicates some kind of plasma is held within these blobs of energy. But we are not sure how they originate, why they seem to interact physically with the surroundings, or they can cause electromagnetic disturbances that have a deep effect on the consciousness of people in close proximity.

Yes – perhaps - aliens might really be coming here in cases like Alan's. They may even home in on these window areas. However, that is mostly just speculation. We know with more assurance that some baffling reports are caused by these blobs of energy and call them UAP (Unidentified Atmospheric Phenomena) to differentiate from more speculative ideas. An MoD UFO study (the Condign report) agrees and even warns such things in our sky are so unpredictable they pose a genuine threat to air traffic. Hence we should study them better.

There is more interesting news. The Pennines are one of the best 'Window Areas' we know. Here, too, there have been UFO sightings throughout the decades causing all sorts of encounters – from lights cavorting about the sky to full blown 'alien contacts'. In fact there have been more encounters with 'aliens' like the one that Alan describes in this book within 20 miles of Todmorden than in any other part of the UK.

That is surely a clue. And it is a shame that the 'little green men' repartee beloved by the our culture and hyped by the media obscures key facts like this and might have cost a good cop such as Alan his future by tarnishing his reputation by association.

It is sad too that we have not grasped the unique opportunity to study this phenomenon in an area perfectly set – with major universities in Manchester and Sheffield a short drive from active locations. A UFO monitor site with modest funds and proper observational equipment would be simple to create and less weather disrupted than Scandinavia. Sadly, it has never happened because UFOs are still thought a joke rather than a scientific question.

In truth they can add much to our understanding of the universe as I explained in an article on 'The neglected science of UFOs' that a colleague and I persuaded New Scientist to publish at a time when the subject was not being taken seriously – in fact the same period when Alan was being hounded out.

This all leads to a further surprise. UFOs are not a modern phenomenon. The same things that Alan saw in 1980 have been 'up there' for centuries.

Consider reports in and around Pendle Hill near Nelson in Lancashire.

On 9 March 1977, during a wave of activity when the moors were awash with UFOs, an object was seen by two men who dropped off night shift workers from a factory. It was just after 3 am when they saw a large cigar shaped mass with multiple 'burning' colours swirling beneath like molten fire. The UFO moved towards their car and created havoc as engine and lights failed and they were trapped with it hovering right over their heads.

This account is much like that reported at Sharneyford on 4 February 1988 (see page 131). That glowing egg shape had 'a swirling liquid or fire inside with constantly changing patterns'. Both these accounts resemble a plasma – highly energised gaseous matter akin to that found within UAP events by scientists at Hessdalen.

Again these are clues that slot together but are easily ignored by the media assuming that UFOs must be either nonsense or spaceships.

In 1977 in the lee of Pendle Hill that swirling glowing UFO was surrounded by a cloud or mist as it fell towards the stricken car. The men jumped out to escape but felt a heavy pressure in the air on their head and shoulders coming from above. This left them with pounding headaches, damage to their eyes as they watered profusely and left with a tingling on their skin that caused their hair to stand on end.

These things are pointers to an electrical field linked to air pressure connected with this UAP. As it drifted away their car engine returned to life on its own.

In the late 20th century there was only one way such a sighting would get interpreted. The Pendle object became a 'UFO from outer space' in popular imagination. Yet that option is merely a 'guess' that could be right or wrong. A speculative punt at a solution that has just gained popularity but, right or wrong, does not deny the initial existence of what the witness actually *saw*. Something extraordinary *was* up in the sky that night. That is really all that matters..

However, there is an intriguing postscript. Something like the same object described in 1977 was seen over Pendle Hill much earlier in the 20th century – when there was no UFO mystery or any concept of aliens to fit around it. That UFO was reported by two police officers at 2.50 am on 14 August 1914. Described as a 'sausage' shape, and much as in the 1977 sighting, with 'smoke' and something on the underside hidden by a fuzzy glow, it was interpreted according to the very different thinking of the early 20th century.

This was the very start of World War 1 with Germany feared to have secret weapons. So the people of Pendle saw this case as visitors from another *empire* rather than another world. History later showed that Germany had no craft capable of flying over Pendle Hill in 1914 and raids from prototype airships only came later in the war on accessible targets nearer to home.

What is important here is to grasp how the same phenomenon was witnessed across many decades by different people. They described it consistently as a still recognisable event – but we, as a society, interpreted those accounts according to the mood of the day and matched it to the latest technical possibilities of that age.

The UFO seen was real and up there, but our thinking about its origin evolved with the state of our own technology and cultural expectations.

In this context it is no surprise that living as we do in an age where NASA is discovering Earth like planets across the universe and exploring mountains on Mars by driving rovers controlled from Earth that our modern society would interpret 'things up in the sky' nowadays as having an alien origin.

If we can go out there then, we argue, they can come here. Indeed, perhaps they can, but should we not pause just in case this is the 21st century 'guess' about an age old riddle that is equally vulnerable to being wrong?

Hopefully you are starting to see that UFO cases are far from a straight choice between doubting the sanity of a witness, or proclaiming an invasion by visiting spaceships that hijack folks from a sleepy town.

Strong, reliable UFO cases like Alan's prove conclusively that a real phenomenon is happening. Hoaxes, lies and delusion do occur, of course, but are surprisingly rare – under 1 % of cases documented in fact. We can speculate all we like as to the cause of the rest – and it is great fun doing so with exotic theories - but in some sense UFOs *are* real and are out there.

Pendle Hill is, of course, also famous as the home of spooky goings on blamed in the early 17th century on local women wrongly accused of practising witchcraft. This was the 'go to' interpretation of that century for things up in the sky - the 400 year old equivalent of blaming an alien invasion.

Interestingly, witchcraft was at the time also believed to locally 'spook cattle' by creating demonic visions that stampede them out of fields to reappear elsewhere. A theme we see incarnated in its space age guise during Alan's account hundreds of years later. It seems tempting to replace demons and witchcraft with aliens and spacecraft and ask which one is correct.

Or, perhaps, we should consider if *both* are wrong!

As yet we cannot fly to worlds further afield where life is probable but we do suppose that aliens coming here are far beyond our abilities and so can make such a trip. Indeed we might argue they study us at a distance, parading in front of us in peculiar guises, possibly taking us aboard for a closer look before returning us home whilst avoiding any clear revelation of their presence.

It is not hard to draw parallels with how our own scientists go into a community of great apes and watch them without being obtrusive, whilst occasionally taking some away for study, putting them back and monitoring progress without interfering with their development. As these apes have intelligence but not enough to understand the methods we use, just how would they interpret the kidnap and befuddled images of being taken into a medical truck whilst samples are extracted and they groggily get returned home? Is there a thriving sub culture of Great Ape lore about strange vehicles from 'beyond' and hairless beings with magical abilities?

Flipping that argument, perhaps an alien David Attenborough is filming human 'abduction' and on another world 'Planet Earth' exists but as a very different kind of alien watched TV show.

It is quite easy to create a theory like this, but that is all we are doing - imagining. Being a neat parallel and filling a satisfying gap is tantalising but it is not proof.

The idea that some UFOs are alien craft needs persuasive evidence to confirm or deny it. That conclusive evidence has long evaded us – in terms of unworldly DNA or non-terrestrial samples of metal or materials. But is that because we have just not found it yet, or it has been spirited away and 'covered up' by secret forces or just because it does not really exist?

One thing stands out from this review of decades of UFO research. The interpretation of what we see in the sky is always changing. Yet the phenomenon remains the same. We have to study the phenomenon and not the interpretation society temporarily places onto it.

Also worth considering is something most people do not realise about the UFO mystery. The shape of a 'flying saucer' seen in movies and on TV - the very symbol of what you think a UFO obviously must 'look like' – is a myth based initially on a cock up!

A pilot flying over the Cascade Mountains in the USA on 24 June 1947 saw what he thought was a formation of advanced military jets and reported this to a local journalist on landing. He spoke of aircraft that were *moving* like a saucer 'skipping' across water. He was likening it to how we toss a flat stone over a pond and see how many times we can get it to 'bounce'. Arnold was here describing the *motion* – NOT the *shape* – of what he was watching. But an enterprising news source with one eye for a catchphrase called these things 'flying saucers' by abbreviating Arnold's words in an accidentally misleading way.

And that error instantly created the image of a saucer *shaped* object that has burrowed deep into human consciousness ever since.

Had Arnold said they moved like stones skipping across water we could now have a culture of rounded pebble objects in science fiction movies and THAT is what most readers would presume a UFO looks like. It would be equally wrong because stone shaped would still not be a description of the form of Arnold's UFO.

Think deeper on this. Hardly any UFOs have ever been reported as skipping through the air in the way that Arnold was actually describing what he watched. Because that was not what the world was *conditioned* to expect from the misreporting of his words. Arnold thought he saw new design military aircraft with crescent like wings and yet, notice, that shape did not become a template for people's ideas of what a UFO should look like either.

A concept of a saucer shaped craft was embedded into popular thinking by a small wrong emphasis of wording, then hyped by countless movies and cartoons until it became iconic. UFOs themselves come in a wide range of shapes – and the one that you might expect to dominate – a saucer – is relatively uncommon.

What does this imply? Popularisation acts as a contaminant and can be easily moulded to reinforce one unusual feature over another through media influence, but this just adds flavouring to a consistent series of events. Those events do happen and their essence remains obvious even when distorted via fads and fashions sprinkled on top by expectation.

Now to the hard part – the cases where credible witnesses like Alan report an extraordinary event described as a constructed object with physical and physiological side effects. What can this be?

It may do damage to a road surface or cause the air to fill with electrical charge and stall car engines, effect radio transmission, make the skin tingle and leave marks and damage on a human body. These cases have consistent details and many thousands of them are on record from almost every place on Earth.

It is true that powerful plasmas might do some of those things. But can they bounce car headlights off a metal surface, relocate cattle and cause 'missing time' where you wake up further down a road? This seems less likely.

These close encounters also reveal trends and patterns that evolve through promotion by our culture. There are hints from Alan's hypnosis that some detail and sounds he saw aboard the 'craft' may have been inspired subconsciously by popular TV shows such as *Dr Who* and *Buck Rogers.* And names and other details likely did seep out from his inner mind whilst 'under the influence'. I have seen this happen in close encounters.

But this does *not* mean that the experience itself should be distrusted even if hypnosis is fallible.

I have serious reservations about regression. It can facilitate recall, but also dredge up images from your mind that are not true memory but may feel like one.

Perhaps some images truly are repressed memories of the UFO event itself. But how are you going to know for sure? In a subject as fraught with cultural influence as this is seems unwise to introduce a voluntary route toward deeper confusion by hypnotising witnesses.

Alan to his credit saw this immediately and has always been careful to separate out what he consciously remembers. And I have no doubt that something physically real was present over the road and did render Alan temporarily 'out of it'. That UFO then led to his disorientation and relocation without recall of how or why. This is more than enough to consider extraordinary possibilities for what happened to him that night but that must be alongside the need to eliminate sober ones first.

Even 'alien contacts' are not immune from the forensic analysis we must give all cases. They *can* have explanations. I have seen an 'alien' turn out to be a telegraph pole silhouetted against the moon, or a cow with light reflecting off its eyes. We should be dragged kicking and screaming towards accepting something more revolutionary such as kidnap by beings from space.

But, of course, we should also accept that it might just be possible and not run away from the 'impossible'.

We saw earlier how some UAP seem to result from rare atmospheric plasmas. Geophysical forces in rocks found in the Pennines can also emit electrical particles under stress and extrude bursts of energy into the atmosphere leaked via things such as TV masts. These so called 'Earthlights' have been seen rising skyward around the Pennine window on several occasions. Might they have enough power to create a close encounter?

Research into the interaction of energy in the atmosphere on the human brain has also revealed that it can change our state of consciousness. Some people get headaches just when thunderstorms close in. More powerful forces up there can make people react even more oddly. One researcher in the USA has developed a device which can induce an electrified UFO sighting. Test subjects wear a 'helmet' that immerses them in a strong energy field simulating a real close encounter and they describe altered states of consciousness and visions and some of the things reported by witnesses like Alan.

These theories are promising opportunities for research. But trying to resolve any case means we must start at the beginning by asking whether an *Identified* solution can exist that might explain what Alan saw? It was the first thing we did in the Manchester group.

I rule out a hoax because my experience says that Alan is describing what he saw. Moreover, I have experience of his evidence reported in this story and heard tapes of the events. So I know his story is truthful.

But there is one new piece of evidence to add - the testimony of Yorkshire bus driver Bob Coates, who came forward in 2014 after hearing that Alan was to give a lecture in town to raise money for charity.

'*Hi, Jenny'*, Bob said to me when I first made contact afterward. '*I was on that road at 5 am. The same time as this was happening to Alan Godfrey*'.

The Todmorden police were contacted hours after Alan's sighting by someone who saw an object passing over Burnley Road near Cliviger around the time of Alan's encounter. But sadly, the local press story days later seems to have stopped them coming forward for fear of ridicule. So having a new back-up witness even as late as 2014 was vital. As we see Bob was driving on Burnley Road around the same time as Alan.

Bob told me he was passing Mons Mill on his right, near where Alan Godfrey saw the UFO in his patrol car. It seemingly was about 4.55 am. Here is what the bus driver saw :

'*All the litter and twigs on the road ahead of me were blowing like a whirlwind. The swirling was very unusual. Higher up the trees nothing was moving. But lower down on trees and bushes and the road* ***all*** *this stuff was.*'

Bob stopped right next to this bizarre sight and in the glow from streetlights saw that there was a blow dried circle on the road:

'It was not the fact that the surface was a big dry patch that alerted me. Instead it was all the twigs in a strange pattern that drew me to look. But closer up I saw the road was swirled dry. I stopped the bus right in the middle of it.'

Because of the earlier rain the road was mostly wet, but not in this swirl patterned area: *'The dry patch went from one side of the road to the other...possibly over the river but I could not see that far'* (The Calder is immediately to the side of the road behind a wall between here and the park, where Alan found the cows).

Bob stopped his bus for a minute but could not get out because he was heading empty to pick up the driver of the 5.10 am bus from Tod to Halifax. This man was waiting at the village of Portsmouth further along Burnley Road. Bob had to get him back to the depot at Millwood to leave on time so was only able to wind down his cab window and briefly stick a hand outside.

'The updraft was amazing. It was NOT a wind blowing at me like a stormy day. The draft was going upwards from off the road into the sky. But it only went up to about 4 feet. I moved my arm above shoulder height and there was nothing at all. The trees here were very still. So I moved my arm back down and the strong updraft was still there hitting me.'

Bob reluctantly left this phenomenon to go pick up the other driver, but quickly turned around and passed the spot again minutes later on the way back toward the depot. There was now no sign of anything odd but he could not stop. It would now be just after 5 am given the bus from Millwood left on time.

The most logical conclusion is that Alan was there about 5/10 minutes *after* Bob drove back toward the depot. It would seem that Alan watched Bob pass through Tod centre as he always claimed he saw a bus before he left to look for the cows. We know that Alan did not leave Tod to head out until after 5.00 am as he talked to an officer who only booked off shift then so driving down Burnley Road around 5.10 am as Alan has long reported fits what Bob now says. I had put Alan's testimony of seeing a bus pass on record in 1982 long before Bob came forward to tell his story.

Bob had to be driving from Mons Mill to Portsmouth and back around 4.55 to 5.05, but Alan and his patrol car could not be at this location during this time given he left Tod later. Indeed the two would have had to pass each other *twice* at some point on Burnley Road if they were ever at the site around the same moment because Bob only stopped there on his way out of Tod and quickly headed back into town, whereas Alan's testimony puts him on Burnley Road for some time after Bob would have got back to the depot with the driver of the bus that left at 5.10.

Neither man says they passed each other on Burnley Road even once, supporting this timeline.

A bus was always the first explanation we had to consider because Alan has always said his own first thought on spotting the UFO was 'It's a bus'. He spoke those words under hypnosis too – hence why it has long been theorised that he possibly *did* see a bus, even before Bob Coates came forward to show that a bus was actually briefly stopped at that same point on the road. Certainly a coincidence that seems to support that idea.

However, Alan immediately changed his mind when closing on the UFO and seeing its full shape. The hypnosis sees him saying: *'It's a bus'* .. *'It's **not** a bus'*, a firm emphasis reacting in fear as he appreciates the truth.

Bob told me he also does not believe Alan saw a bus, because: *'Given the timings, if it was a bus then it had to be **my** bus as I was the only one on the road.....and what I saw out there truly was something strange.'*

We also have three independent witnesses to part of the case (including PC Agley that Alan took back to the spot immediately after the sighting). They *all* saw the swirled dry circle on the highway and the debris on the surface. Both Alan and Bob saw the effects of the strange wind as it happened on site and Bob *felt* the upward suction linked to that swirl.

So there is very clear evidence that a *real* phenomenon happened as they are all describing it. And given that it was at the same location as the UFO at more or less the same time then these events must be linked in some way. A bus alone cannot explain all that as Bob's bus obviously did not create what he himself witnessed.

However, only Alan saw the UFO itself. Of course, there is the untraced witness at Cliviger and Leonard Smith, the caretaker at the school who told Alan what he saw over the road. Smith told me that something bright was moving across the valley near where he now knows Alan stopped. It zig zagged back and forth a few times and then streaked away over the hills.

If we take these things together they do connect a glowing object *in the sky* with the marks on the road around the same time and, of course, buses do not fly.

I asked Alan what he thought of this possibility.

He told me: '*The theory is full of holes and laughable. For this to work the bus would have had to be sideways across the carriageway for me to see the full five upper deck windows that I saw on the UFO.*'

Bob confirmed to me that he did not park sideways.

Alan added: '*The object spanned the full road width. If any service bus leaving town had gone sideways across the highway and I had come up to it with my blue flashing lights ablaze I am sure the driver would have got out and come over to me to explain why it was in that position completely blocking the road.*'

That seems a telling argument - however, Alan can demolish the theory that he saw a bus in an even more powerful way. He used to drive one!

'Before joining the police I worked as a bus driver from that same Metro depot. I drove the very buses sceptics supporting this theory say I mistook on both day and night. I knew what they looked like. I would have recognised one even in the dark.'

So, if we rule out the bus as cause then what else might this UFO be?

In the years leading up to Alan's encounter our Manchester group investigated a spate of sightings on the hills around Rossendale and Todmorden in which a gliding, silent, dark object would emerge out of low cloud and glow an eerie red before heading south with just a rushing noise and powerful lights. Plotting the data we discovered a pattern, both for its course and how reports were happening around 2 am on a Saturday morning.

UFOs do not fly on timetables, so we immediately suspected that something that did was being witnessed. But it made no sense of the observations, which included a senior police officer from Greater Manchester scared witless when this UFO swooped over his head as he stood on a moor near Bury. Of course, we knew that Alan's sighting was also in the early hours of a Saturday.

The investigation that we undertook was one of the most interesting I have been involved with, because it needed lots of deduction followed by a field experiment to try to prove the working theory that we developed.

It took weeks to pull this together but we eventually came to the conclusion that what was being seen was a commercial cargo flight that for a strange reason appeared unlike any aircraft to those underneath

So we set a trap to catch a UFO and mounted investigators on the tops around Bacup and Todmorden on one of those early Saturdays when we knew this flight was due. We had help from air traffic controllers who recognised that we were trying to solve this puzzle sensibly and who were also concerned by the possibility. Indeed they allowed one of our team to join a location where flights were tracked on radar. When that cargo flight was detected heading south up on the moors we were on look out.

This experiment proved a success. The aircraft – a flight from Scotland operated by a major international carrier – was engaging in a scary practice. The crew were throttling back engines, switching off lights other than the tail fin logo, and almost 'gliding' over the Pennines giving the crew a nice view all around. It is not clear if they were aware that their activities were triggering UFO reports on the ground as they approached population centres and had to power up engines and lights resulting in a frightening illusion when seen from below.

After our stake-out established this plane was masquerading as a UFO the airport and airline 'had words' and the matter was amicably resolved. One spate of UFO sightings came to an end – solved by our UFO group.

Ironically, this investigation was immortalised by the long running ITV series – *Heartbeat* – set around the fictional police force at a small Yorkshire town. Heartbeat told me that their script was 'inspired' by reading an account of our investigation, but, sadly, the hard work we did was cut from the fictional recreation.

In fact the Heartbeat episode solved the case when a single police officer did what we took months to do. The scene at the end where the copper tries to convince his disbelieving inspector of this 'explanation' is amusing. But most of the audience watching likely found the notion of a 'gliding cargo plane' absurd.

Yet the story was true!

This same TV series gave an accolade to Alan Godfrey's encounter also – an episode where an officer had a close encounter in his patrol car. Alan even served as adviser. So Heartbeat is probably the only UK drama series with two separate episodes based on real life UFO cases and they both happened around Todmorden!

This 'naughty' cargo flight was a success for our detective skills at MUFORA but proved not to be what Alan saw because that plane was not airborne that night.

So if he did not mistake a bus, or a plane, what about imagining a UFO based on the design of the Futuro modal house, as some sceptics have long proposed? They did so because of the superficial similarity of shape between both objects but this is irrelevant given the other witnesses who shared part of the sighting such as physical evidence seen on the road. No illusion of a future house can create that.

The next thing we considered fits much better with the strange vortex felt by Bob Coates over Burnley Road and the swirling dry of the road surface seen by him, Alan and PC Agley. For here we have clear multiple witness accounts of that effect and its aftermath.

Editor of the Journal of Meteorology, Dr Terence Meaden, has worked with me on cases of similar effects found in crop field from the early 1980s. These were being blamed by the excitable media on aliens and called 'crop circles'. But most of them were hoaxes and the few that were not had been reported long before the press got interested. We had cases back to the 1940s and reports feature in science journals even in the 19th century.

Meaden theorised as the cause of these swirls a 'plasma vortex' – a stationary tornado. Given the links to plasma found in UFO events and the vortex seen over Burnley Road, I also found it potentially relevant to close encounters. Paul Fuller and I collated evidence and presented it to an Oxford conference of physicists from the UK, USA and Japan including Terence Meaden.

It seemed possible that this idea of an atmospheric plasma creating swirled circles in fields may trigger UFO sightings, which is what Paul Fuller and I argued in our 1990 book 'Crop Circles: A Mystery Solved?'

This plasma vortex is a very rare atmospheric anomaly but often happens in valleys by hills after a passing frontal system. In the right conditions it produces a low level stationary tornado. That vortex can rotate very fast – swirling dry road surfaces and causing other damage – and generates sufficient energy to trigger electrical disturbances nearby – such as police radios or car electrics, but not to diesel buses. If such a thing was observed by a passer-by then the rotating vortex of debris being sucked upwards might resemble a UFO.

Reasonably, Alan thinks that the 'vortex' he saw was *caused* by the object hovering above. But could an extreme weather event have formed both things? Was the debris picked up off trees and the road via the powerful suction felt when Bob held his hand out of his cab becoming what looked like a UFO by the time that Alan had reached the scene?

The weather data for that night in Todmorden shows the heavy rain reported by Alan was from a departing Arctic air stream. This cleared just before the sighting and an intense anticyclone arrived from the north-west. Meaden says this fits well with his pattern of atmospherics predicting formation of a plasma vortex.

Of course, in Todmorden air pressure would not flatten a solid road surface like it could do a crop field but was able to swirl dry the water on top. By daylight this effect would have evaporated quickly, unlike in fields where crop stays 'set' by the damage for days.

I expect some readers will find this idea rather absurd and I do not blame them. I was pretty sceptical of this possibility myself until I investigated a case in Marple, Cheshire at 11 am on 15 June 1988.

Roy Sandbach and I published findings for TORRO – the Tornado Research centre that advises places such as power plants in the UK to guard against storm damage. This case had multiple independent witnesses in daylight to reveal things that are not otherwise obvious.

Marple is in the south of the Pennine hills and is similar to Tod with a steep valley rising north and eastward, and sloping south west towards Stockport. Then in the middle is a narrow strip with the Peak Forest canal and River Goyt to hem in fields and villages as the Calder does in Todmorden.

At 11 am in a local primary school the headmaster saw through his office window loose 'grass' rising in clumps from the field beside the boundary.

Suspecting children were tossing it in play he went to stop them, but when he arrived it had ceased and the children were on the school side of the fence saying that they had watched it rise into the air on its own.

He was naturally sceptical but at 12.45 pm the head was supervising a lunchtime game of rounders when he and several children saw the phenomenon at close range as clumps of hay rose up again just 100 feet away.

It was climbing skyward camera side of the fence seen below, spiralling anti clockwise to roof height.

These clumps began to stick together as they continued rotating and formed a dark oval mass looking very like a 'UFO' - as the kids excitedly shouted. It seemed completely solid at this point and would have surely been reported as a structured craft if its earlier 'creation' had not been witnessed. As they all watched in amazement this oval - about 20 feet in diameter - hovered over the field before moving south west above school grounds across their heads.

It disappeared over the top of a church moving down slope in the direction of Hazel Grove.

I quizzed witnesses about their experience as it passed overhead and they referred to feeling odd and a 'strange tingle' in the air as the oval mass passed above, suggesting an electrical charge surrounding them. It kept coherence as a 'structured object' until lost out of sight.

Interestingly the headmaster also described a downward pressure pushing on head and shoulders gently forcing them into the ground when directly above.

Roy and I found independent witnesses who had not seen the 'UFO' form or knew what occurred at the school. They were in nearby houses and minutes later saw the shape lose coherence, break up and drop to the ground as the disintegrating object fell on the slope.

These physical effects match what the witnesses at Nelson reported during that March 1977 UFO incident and suggest a balance of forces within the vortex with upward motion (as felt by Bob in Tod and revealed at Marple when it 'sucked up' the hay) and downward pressure felt pushing onto the head also. These eventually equalised and when in balance the UFO could 'hover' and moved sideways riding air currents.

Clearly this Marple event was caused by some kind of atmospheric vortex but had many of the same effects described by close encounter witnesses who saw UFOs.

The Marple object was only identifiable because witnesses saw it form and others saw it break apart. If it had been dark or only the middle of the event seen then this case could be a baffling close encounter like Alan's.

Something like this excites the scientist in me every bit as much as finding aliens would do. But readers will still be dubious that Alan's sighting can be explained as a fancy weather phenomenon. Although tornadoes can and do form regularly in the UK in the right conditions.

But what of the missing time, relocated cows, marks on Alan's leg, damage to his boot, how he suddenly found himself further down Burnley Road and the story told under hypnosis involving Yosef, robots and much else? Despite the attraction of the parallels with the Marple case these added factors must give caution. And I stress that all I am doing here by positing this plasma theory is show how UFO researchers try to reach the truth by eliminating all rational answers first.

You investigate and eliminate the obvious solutions, then the less obvious but still within the realms of science and only if and when all these fail against the evidence do you consider the extraordinary. Even then it will always be a balance of probabilities.

Most attacks on the credibility of a witness stem not from doubts over their honesty but suspicion over the extreme nature of what we are then presumed to have to believe in order to accept their story.

Alan has never said he saw aliens or even that he knows what he witnessed. I admire that honesty. Even if he did encounter aliens we should not attack his credibility, of course, but if he did chance instead upon a rare scientific anomaly then it would still be amazing and might defuse much of the subsequent disrespect.

Having looked at the more down to earth options that MUFORA considered - what about this concept of an alien contact? Could it *really* have happened?

Whilst I was not directly involved in the hypnosis experiments I have viewed footage of all sessions and met both doctors who worked with Alan.

I was also hypnotised myself to a light in the sky that I saw in Chester in August 1977. I believed then that it was a low flying aircraft but wanted to experience regression to that event to understand the process. My session brought out checkable facts that I had long forgotten but were later proven true through written records. But just as much of what I said under regression was nonsense. After viewing old calendars I gave the day of the week incorrectly when asked during hypnosis so must have just guessed it wrongly under pressure.

There are good reasons why hypnosis is not trusted in court as evidence to help solve traumatic crimes. What Alan describes in his regression about 'alien abduction' is undeniably fascinating but its extraordinary nature gives it prominence out of all proportion to its reliability. It also downgrades the consciously recalled facts which have a more solid foundation.

Whilst none of this means that Alan's account of his time 'inside' the UFO is all imaginary, it puts it on a different level to data not coming from hypnosis.

Alan said to me in 1982 as we sat together at Harry Harris's home watching the final regression video for the first time – *'I cannot be sure of the origin or the credibility of these images I just 'saw' under hypnosis when 'inside the UFO'*. I agree with his caution.

Of course, I am very aware that the possibility of alien life is even more likely today given our discovery of multiple potentially habitable planets around nearby stars seemingly announced by astronomers every few weeks now that we have new technology for the search.

I have certainly investigated enough close encounters to agree that something very strange is going on and would never rule out that aliens might be coming to visit us. Distrusting hypnosis does not change that.

More to the point - if there is intelligence involved in the UFO encounter apart from our own then it need not come from a distant planet. There are possibilities emerging from modern science, such as a parallel reality.

Physics is now much more open to the thought that multiple dimensions or layers of universe interact with one another alongside the one we call home. If there are beings living in such locations then some may have a way to slip sideways through cracks between these multiverses – perhaps making use of those atmospheric forces to serve as a gateway - those alive in the Pennine window. If so the problems crossing the galactic void when limited by the speed of light might disappear.

Heather Dixon, who now does the job that I once did coordinating UFO investigations for the British UFO Research Association, told me of a case on the evening of 15 July 1995 at a garden barbecue near Hebden Bridge. She investigated with a local medic.

A husband, wife and two others who all requested anonymity reported a strange sensation where time and space got distorted and local sounds suddenly faded into silence. They then saw strange lights that came at them from an object in the form of bright beams which lead to a jump in time of over an hour. After this all witnesses were left with jumbled memories.

It was as if they were having 'blinks' in reality where things that had existed, such as a glass, vanished and were no longer part of the surroundings afterward. One witness described it as time being like a video tape that got sliced up and stuck together again as a confused mix that nobody agreed upon and not what it was like before. Reality had broken into multiple strands of time and space when the UFO 'beamed' light at them.

Something is causing more than its fair share of such bizarre experiences tied in with light shows in the Pennines. Often these are understandably interpreted as an 'alien contact'. But does the unusual physics of this location attract visitors through gaps in the multiverse thanks to local energy splintering boundaries?

Perhaps and something not dissimilar is being explored by long time Pennine UFO researcher Nigel Mortimer in his fascinating series of 'portal' books.

What we do know is that often during close encounter cases witnesses seem to enter an altered state of consciousness that leads to missing time. I call it the 'Oz Factor', as it is like Dorothy temporarily visiting the land of Oz - via a tornado in that fable, of course.

But if some physically real force can appear, conk out car engines, induce an energy field surrounding a witness, put them into 'stasis' and trigger a halt to memory until they 'come to' confused or located elsewhere then an Oz Factor state is the key.

Witnesses understandably seek answers to fill a gap in time via hypnosis. They reasonably assume that the unrecalled period had actual events, so a narrative emerges from their subconscious to fill the blanks. But what if they were just unconscious during this lost time?

Many witnesses who undergo close encounters have a history of odd things happening from early childhood. They see lights playing around their cots and have unexplained 'time jumps' during life. Many around Tod have told me they have experienced things like this.

However in 2008 I too awoke in the night feeling very strange with a sense of terror. Next thing I knew I was on the floor gazing upward, totally disorientated.

I started to crawl away and was violently sick. Then I lost consciousness before waking up in bed what turned out to be some time later. At first I thought that I had dreamt all this, but my bathroom proved I had really been sick. So I had just had my very own 'time lapse'.

Had this happened outside or there been a bright light shining through my window I might have been persuaded to probe into that period wiped from my memory. Instead I called my doctor who diagnosed vaso vagal syncope (VVS) caused by a sudden drop in blood pressure along the vagus nerve. Many things can trigger such attacks including stress, lack of sleep and – interestingly - a bright light. VVS prone people have 'blackouts' sporadically throughout life without warning or usually any awareness of their cause. Indeed I had four or five other examples years apart back to childhood but had never recognised them as such before.

So there can be a medical cause for 'missing time' with you just 'out of it' and no events to recover. But if I was regressed to seek them unaware I had VVS some might be 'created' by my mind?

Another clue comes from 'observed abductions'.

It is very rare for a witness who, like Alan, experiences a period of missing time and recalls being 'abducted', to be seen by strangers during that spell of unconsciousness. But if another person chances to be in the vicinity and does not share in their close encounter what do they see of the witness who gets 'abducted'?

There appears to be a proximity zone round the UFO – inside of which you fully experience the reality distorting effects from whatever causes the close encounter. If you are further away then you seem immune to any influence.

It seems that nobody was close to Alan after he was struck by that flash of light before he awoke in his patrol car further down Burnley Road. So where was he really located during that period? Was he semi-conscious but still in his car or aboard the UFO as hypnosis implies?

From admittedly very few cases where passers-by see an abductee in the midst of this 'missing time' we have clues. One being that secondary witness see the UFO as glows or energy and rarely as a craft. The person beyond the clutch of the Oz Factor also does not experience time distortion. Yet if this observer sees the 'abducted' witness as they pass by, almost none report them being carried into a UFO, just see them 'in a daze' where they were at the point of last conscious memory.

This suggests that perhaps the 'abductee' is immobilised and semi-conscious by whatever causes the UFO whilst they experience missing time. Indeed one passer-by who tried to help a witness considered them very deep asleep because he could not wake them up.

Is that 'deep sleep' the memory gap that gets filled in later by hypnotic recall? And is the memory retrieved an actual event or a dream during that unconsciousness – full of alien imagery perhaps because it follows directly the sighting of what you believed was a UFO?

In summary:- We do not know if Alan ever entered the UFO that he saw, but I am positive he did see one.

We do not know if it even was a craft or if a period of missing time exists other than lost awareness.

We cannot know if Alan was just in a state of shock - as anyone in his position would be - or whether the bright flash of light somehow switched his consciousness or shifted his space-time reality.

The gaps plugged by hypnosis stem from assuming there is a memory to find, but the mind will create something if there is no gap. Nature abhors a vacuum, so if you form one by accident something will try to fill it.

It is possible that Alan Godfrey *was* abducted by some force or entity, but even if not the UFO he saw was undeniably real. Abduction experiences certainly occur to trustworthy people on some sort of level.

But the state of consciousness and the cause of that experience remain open to debate.

As a UFO researcher I prefer caution to undue speculation but my scepticism over the involvement of aliens does not diminish my total respect for Alan.

Nor does it alter my certainty that he had a quite remarkable experience.

I would be delighted if my caution proves wrong, because the reality of alien contact would be a world changing event. Either way it is thanks to people like Alan coming forward that we can even ask such profound questions.

So whatever you think happened applaud him for having the guts to tell his story in this book. And try to summon up that same courage over your experience if you kept it secret. Because it will almost certainly help to talk to others who understand what you went through.

The theories posed in this review may all prove wrong but this remains the greatest riddle of the 21st century. By resolving that mystery we could learn so much about the world around us or unravel the boundaries of time and space. Any of those things would bring unknown benefits for future generations.

Of course, establishing the existence of aliens – especially ones with greater knowledge than us – would quite simply be the biggest event in all our lifetimes.

So just the chance this happened on a wet night on Burnley Road should excite every reader. Because Alan's story could change everything we know - forever.

Jenny Randles October 2017

Have you seen something unusual in the sky?

If you wish to contact the author and share your thoughts on his experience or would like to describe (in confidence if you prefer) something that has happened to you, then you can do so via:-

www.ozfactorbooks.com

10 Marton Green, Stockport, Cheshire SK3 8LT

nufon@btinternet.com